25 and Self-ish

BRITTANY BERGER

Bookbaby
7905 N. Crescent Blvd
Pennsauken, NJ 08110
www.bookbaby.com

Printed in the Unites States of America

ISBN: 978-1-54392-922-5 (print)

ISBN: 978-1-54392-923-2 (ebook)

Cover Photograph by Sean Michael McCabe

Author Photograph by Sean Michael McCabe

Edited by Eleanor Embry

CONTENTS

Romance 1

   Summer 2015 2

   Saturday 35

   The First Kiss 44

   The Last Kiss 73

Resignation 103

   Tunnel Vision 104

   The Medium 129

Resilience 151

   Brexit 152

   The Silver Platter 189

   Jumping Ship 218

Rebirth 243

   Just Do It 244

Dedication

To all of those who feel stuck in their lives, fear not.

The solution is now in your hands.

Acknowledgements

I am grateful to all of those who:

Continually listen to my *long stories* that I can never seem to shorten.

Supported me as I lived through this journey and when I decided to write about it.

My mom who has *always* believed in me and never allowed me to stop dreaming.

My dad who instilled in me a strong work ethic, pushing me, thankfully, not out of the house.

JK, for being my first best friend and taking part in this adventure of realization.

MD, for introducing me to the greatest love story of my life to date.

BM, for discovering my strengths and believing in me, before I believed in myself.

MC, for being my sunshine in the rain and always having my back.

SB, for seeing past my age on the first day of work and filling my spirit until the last day.

*Y*S, for existing as my spiritual soul sister, fueling my fire in every area of my being.

*M*P, for gifting me with the opportunity to experience positive change and personal growth.

*E*E, the universe brought us together for a reason and its result turned out to be beautiful.

*R*obin, for being my guardian angel and living within my heart. Your spirit is always with me.

*T*he Medium, who predicted this project would come to fruition and without ever being able to imagine, she was right.

I am most grateful to the *u*niverse for guiding me on this path to live and speak my truth. I am thankful for having had the chance to live through this journey of learning to be self-*ish*.

I thank the universe for these messages,
Trusting my intuition.
That there is no rush in time.
That you are exactly where you need to be.
That you are everything you need to be for yourself.
You are right on time.

Love,

B

Romance

Summer 2015

In one year, I will have survived the first quarter of my life. I hope that when the day comes, the universe gives me an A+ for one hell of an effort.

As toddlers our parents enroll us in swim classes where we learn how not to drown. This is the first obstacle to our natural independence, learning how to stay afloat as miniature broods. Not until we turn twenty-five do we realize the *real* struggle of staying afloat. That life does *not* get easier; it gets harder. Then comes the time when we acknowledge, I am twenty-five. Am I in crisis mode or survival mode? And where are my floaties when I need them?

This period of turning twenty-five is generationally identified as a *crisis for twenty somethings*. I don't want to fall in that norm. I always play it safe. I never take risks and I always feel in control. Approaching this age, I realize just being comfortable and content isn't going to be enough for me. Swimming solo into the real world, I came to realize I couldn't bring my floaties with me. So, will I continue to stay afloat past the milestone known as my mid-twenties? I want to prosper in this "crisis" instead of drowning in it. But where do I begin in this journey to survival?

Since I have yet to take time off in over a year, my best friend, Jilly, gifted me one solution. A vacation. So simple, yet so not when working a full time corporate job. But when she told me the vacation was free, I was all in. I had heard that the best things in life are free, and I wanted a taste of that.

Once I enrolled in the post-college work field of adulthood, I found it difficult to keep a constant thread of communication. Especially when an hour of my day is willed to Equinox, there is minimum nine hours of my time dedicated to everything but talking to the squad. Since I was a focused worker from an early age, I discovered using Gchat very late in the game. Now, we can exchange life complaints about hating our jobs, the latest gossip of "*she's engaged to who?!*" and assist in the final decisions of items stored in our online shopping carts, while not having to worry about substituting my date night with Shonda Rhymes watching Scandal.

After realizing my best friend and I have not spent more than four consecutive days together since she moved to New York, Jilly devised a brilliant plan to take a cost friendly, practically free two-week vacation together abroad. Since thousands of people apply for this trip, I never thought we would be chosen, especially because we have visited this country before. But we were proven wrong when fate followed behind and surprisingly chose us to partake. We are the type of gals who never win anything in life and that day, our time finally came.

To other fellow Jew crews, this trip is popularly known as Birthright. *Birthright is a non-for profit educational organization*

*that sponsors a free ten-day cultural trip of sightseeing and tour-
ing historical cities in Israel, for young adults of Jewish heritage.*
Learning about our Jewish history is important to us. But in
our eyes, burying our faces in large amounts of hummus, and
letting fresh, chocolate rugelach melt down our chins was the
real heritage we were interested in.

On a scale of 1-10, what could be better than food? Nothing.
But second best in the competition would naturally be, men.
And not just any men, but Israeli *soldiers*, who are enlisted in
the army and yet still volunteer to participate on a part of the
voyage we, forty total strangers, call holiday. Our bus creeps to
a halt in front of the stop where five militias wait in their uniforms before hopping onboard our lorry.

Eager to selfishly magnify the view, our group leaders make
us pull down the shades so the soldiers don't feel uncomfortable with forty sets of human eyes staring at them through the
windows. Do you think that could stop me? Of course not.
I peep through the center of two shades and try to catch my
drool over two of the soldiers waiting to get on the bus. They
basically just stepped out of a *GQ* magazine: *Special Uniform
Summer Edition*. Customarily, it is younger soldiers, around
eighteen years old dressed in green training uniforms, that are
chosen to partake on our cultural adventure. But we seemed to
have recruited the older, crem de la crem tall, dark, and hand-
somes. Before roll call, our guide reveals that one of the soldiers
is a Pilot in the Air Force and the other, a Commander in the

Navy. Jilly and I meet eyes wide with growing smiles thinking, how did we get so *lucky*? Only God knows.

Since every novel begins with a love story, at least the ones I like to read, it is known that there is always *"an American on Birthright who falls in love with an Israeli soldier on the trip."* I always thought that was bogus because how do you fall in love with someone you just met in a short couple of days? I don't know. Oh wait! I do, because somehow, I – became - that - girl.

There is no reason or past occurrence for this belief but I always thought that whenever I get married, I will be settling. I never thought I would actually meet someone in life that I would wholly, unconditionally love. I guess it's because I haven't met anyone close to that description who made me feel that effervescent. Then again, I am in my hopeful prime, simply selective on an extreme level and choose not to waste my time if time allows it. I believe in more of an instant click than a growth of love. Why? Because like a new handbag, if it stops me in my tracks, I know it's the one and I shall buy it *(Selfridges, Prada Pionerre Bag, Happy Birthday to me)*.

Why do the majority of novels that interest me feature love stories? Because this genre allows me to live vicariously through a love so strong and so deep that I emotionally submerge myself in it. A lot of girls subconsciously or voluntarily want that love story, and people (like me) think they're crazy! I never thought a Nicholas Sparks love actually existed. But then I met Mr. GQ and found out, it really can exist.

Making their debut one after the other, the Pilot appears in dark shades, a light blue button down, navy slacks and army boots. Don't we just love a man in uniform? As he walks down the busway, my assessment begins, "He's tall…and cute…big nose, but still cute. Maybe he's a contender," I note to Jilly.

Next up, in what feels like motion picture slow motion is Mr. GQ, the Commander. He steps onboard and immediately, the whole – world – stops. Like I'm not even kidding. It stops. This guy, coming in at 6'4", tan skin, dark hair, white teeth, takes off his Ray-Bans to reveal ocean blue eyes. As if he is the Dolce & Gabbana model in the Light Blue fragrance commercial, I imaginatively lie with him in the small Italian raft, dressed in white matching bikinis. Sigh. With my x-ray vision I can sense his physique busting through his white custom fit shirt. Jilly is starting to date someone back home but I, being single as a Pringle, was not. So, if I do choose to mingle with these models, I am the flavor of the week in this row. Jilly and I dejectedly exchange looks as if to say, is he a real human? As he walks in the direction of the back of the bus I think to myself, holy crap - he's too hot for me anyway, so in turn, I'll go for the Pilot.

The day continues and I can't help but find ways to catch glimpses of his beauty. I stare from afar behind my headrest until we pull into the gravel at the Banias Falls. Our first destination and first time deplaning the transport with Israelis included. Our group waits as they change into civilian attire and we begin a suspended trail approaching the cascading waterfall.

I scan the area and see the Pilot in my periphery, staring my way. Glimmering a smile, I continue walking until he emerges at my side to introduce himself. Even though I spent eight years at a Jewish Hebrew-Day School, I only remember a small amount of Hebrew (sorry Mom and Dad). Since the Pilot's English wasn't that great, we attempt our best to converse in both holy languages and walk alongside each other for the remainder of the trail. I attempt to ask the secrets of being a Pilot in the Air Force, but Pilots, I find, don't tell their secrets. I learn about his day-to-day flying fighter jets in the desert. He learns about my clearly non-eventful day job where the only place I fly to is the bathroom. Some of the girls on this trip acted as vultures when they saw a soldier. As they flood around us, I remove myself from the frenzy infestation of female hormones, to race Jilly up the rock-leveled steps.

The view of the forest surrounding the spring of water, cascading down into the river, is the epitome of tranquility. How something so beautiful could live in a land that is barren is another one of Israel's marvels. I take in the beauty and the breeze it grants while remembering to take one last photo before walking back to the camp. As I focus the picture perfectly, a hand reaches out in front of my lens and I stop. It's him.

"Want me to take a picture of you in front of it?" he asks.

I stand frozen, unable to find my words, or my breath. I take the picture and walk away, "No thanks, but thanks," I mutter before running off in God's speed. NO THANKS, BUT THANKS?? What kind of response was that! His beauty literally blinds me into a fast walking mime. I have never had an issue talking to a guy before - ever, but he feels like a supernatural Avatar. There are many situations in life where I thought I had a pair of balls, but since I can't find them in this moment he must have stolen them in passing. As a rescue mission for myself, I need to grow a pair real quick before I faint during the next encounter. This awkward feeling is a new reaction to add to my list of firsts.

Returning from the hike, our group sits down at picnic tables to play a game of speed dating with the soldiers. We split up into groups and the five soldiers revolve among us. After sitting in anticipation while talking to the other contestants, next in line is the one and only, Mr. GQ. Yes, to answer your question I died a little inside but as a surprise to myself, I do not faint.

"What do you like to do on the weekends?" Jilly asks.

"I like to go to the beach. BBQ. Spend time by the pool with a glass of wine or whiskey," he aims for my line of sight.

"If you could live anywhere in the world, where would it be?" Dana asks.

"Here. This is my home," he answers.

"If someone handed you $10,000, what is the first thing you would do?" Ryan inquires.

"I would book a vacation with a girl that I liked," he raises his eyebrow in my direction, and I literally start to sweat.

"Why don't you ask me a question now?" he directs to me.

I stop breathing and think…"Chocolate or vanilla?" I ask.

"Chocolate. And you?" he asks.

"I like both. I don't discriminate," I look away as I find the will to breathe and the blush rises to my cheek's surface until I'm saved by the bell. Time is up and the next suitor takes the hot seat.

Every person who comes next is a blur. I can't stop thinking about him. I was never boy crazy in any past admires, especially this early on. There was only one courter before him where I felt a magnetic attraction. Every tested love afterwards was a leisurely growth to a rapid decline of my interest. This magnetic field however trumped any allure I have ever seasoned before. All I can think about is his contagious bright smile, blue eyes, and my heart racing 1,000 beats a minute. Jilly wakes me from my daydream to buy our favorite Magnum ice cream cone to share, my senses awaken because as you can recall, food comes first, boys come second.

Jilly and I are two of the last to return to the bus and I notice him sitting in his original seat from this morning. Before taking my seat we lock eyes and immediately I can feel my heavy breathing, heart pounding against my chest. I don't even know him. Why are my insides oxidizing to this level of pressure? I shift around to get one last view and catch the Pilot's stare mid turn. Ugh. A conundrum. Who do I want? Who do I *not*? I'm not used to this much attention from the highest valued suitors. This is too complicated for me. Jilly, I need my ice cream.

Our next destination is the Jordan River. For those who don't know, the river is kind of grey and, despite being shallow, has a strong enough current for one wave at the end to be considered "rafting." Also known as the sole purpose of this activity. The bus drops us off and the girls walk into our directed dressing rooms to change into our bathing suits. Having to walk in nothing but my pink bathing suit and matching pink water shoes is not what I consider any bit of attractive, but since everyone looks as awkward as I do, I embrace the melting pink icy look.

I search the crowd and pick my four rafters. Jilly used to play water polo, so she is a treading water expert. Dana runs marathons, so she has endurance for any situation. Eliza is a yoga instructor, so she has promising upper body strength. Tifi is our brave Israeli leader who fears nothing, which is important when cautioning nature. And lastly there's me, and I work out, so I'm very confident our team will not flip over and die. As we attempt to close our child-sized life jackets, we emerge into the not so inflatable raft. If you happened to have had a boob job in these tight child sized zip ups, there is a large chance your implants would pop out of their sockets. Luckily for me, I pay a rental fee each month for mine with birth control, so in case of an emergency, I know I will survive.

Fear #1: When it comes to waters that shine the color grey, no matter how hot it is outside I will ~~not~~ never get in the water. I don't know what consistency the bottom of the floor is made of, or what animals may call this home, so I refuse to even have my butt touch the surface. I will *not* fall in.

Jilly and I team lead the paddling until the raft behind us forcefully bumps into our side, gliding us straight into the trees. Fear #2: Unrecognized and inescapable contact with insects. The more we frantically paddle away from the invasion of wild nature, the environment works against us and we drift into closer proximity of spiders spinning winning cobwebs between the leaves.

I shout at my troops to get our shit together and paddle as hard as we possibly can because it's only Day 2 of this trip and our lives depend on it. We cannot get stuck in undiscovered wildlife. I refuse. Just our luck, we get stuck, and I do the only thing I can think of in this small ship of disappointment: bury my head between my knees and pray for a miracle. Sharp tree branches poke our backs until our fearless Tifi jumps into the water and pushes us back into unofficially safe waters, freeing us out of the nook. With enough distance apart, the girls and I attempt to relax while lying across the raft absorbing the sun. There is nothing like the Israeli sun to get a bronze, beautiful bake, another part of my heritage I want to absorb.

Leaning against the raft with my elbows supporting my weight, I feel someone grab my lifejacket and before I can close my mouth from screaming, I'm pulled off and plunged into the water. Yes, I scream like a girl, and yes, the most important thing I care about is my mascara running, but then I see who it is. Mr. GQ.

At first, I was treading water until I realize I can stand. I try to run towards him but the fastest running speed in water is still slow. So did I get anywhere? Not really. Was I already out of breath? Immensely. He starts to swim away until he disappears underneath the grey and the Jaws music sounds in my head. Emerging from under me, he places me on top of his broad muscular shoulders and flips me backwards. You have got to be kidding me. I AM OFFICIALY IN THE MURK. This has become a water-wrestling match I never wanted to be in with no one to tap out. I am out of breath, missing a water shoe and have cloudy, stale water in my mouth and up my nose. My mascaraed face probably looks like a raccoon's. This is anything but romantic.

"It's just water! Don't worry," he jokes. He clearly doesn't know me. Water is not my friend. I try to splash the entire river into his face, and when that doesn't stop him, I wave my white hat to surrender, heavily out of breath. My raft is a football field length in front of us and I don't feel like swimming all the way there.

"Want to be my swimming partner?" he asks.

I splash him in the face, "No. I'm done swimming. I prefer to float my way back." Just like a shark, never rest in the water because when you least expect it, they'll come to getchya. With no other option but to stay in my neutral stance, I see a pink object floating in the water and pray that it is my sister shoe. I swim in its direction and place it on my left foot floating back to my original position. I have to admit, at this point, the water actually feels nice and I am proud of myself for being one with nature. Suddenly, I feel a grip take hold of my foot and screech as I think, given my luck, some type of animal is trying to drown me, but it isn't. It is just him. Again.

"I will guide you," he says. I look to my left and see my friend Jared in lead of his raft trying to splash us. I wiggle out of his hold and lunge at Jared's vest to pull him in and take his place on the mini barge. "Go, go, go!" I yell to his rafters as they paddle forward in the direction of my vessel.

Finally I reach my original transport, exhausted, and hop back inside. The girls begin to slow clap and giggle while I lay there defeated catching my breath with no clean water to sip in sight. Once I finally sit up on the back next to Jilly, another swimmer hops on.

"Nooo!" I yell.

"You left me!" he says.

"What do you mean I left you, you pulled me off to begin with!" I argue.

"Round 2?" he asks.

"No!" I try to push him off the raft but he ends up taking me back with him. Ugh! I can't win. But do I want to? I put my hand out for him to shake, "Truce?"

He laughs and picks me up, throwing me across the river. I wipe my eyes, seeing the final dip coming ahead and swim en route to the raft. Jilly takes my hand and pulls me in, leaving Mr. GQ behind. I lie on my stomach on the back of the raft before the river drops and I bid a Queen's farewell in his direction. If there are three things I have learned, it is that, first and foremost, I am proud of how I handled almost dramatically drowning and being eaten by spiders. Two, that as annoying as being exposed to the unfavorable side of mother nature is, I prized being chosen by his good looks and persistence, and, three, that I could use a well-deserved clean shower, long nap, and a high calorie snack… or two.

After changing back into our clothes, Jilly and I shuffle our tired feet to the bus. Upon sitting down, we reach for our Kind bars, deodorant, and clean & clear oil pads (necessities in 110-degree heat). As we settle into our seats, I feel my eyes slowly collapse in nap preparation until a tap on my shoulder stirs me, "Have room for one more?" I open my eyelids and gaze back towards Jilly. You've got to be kidding me. Jilly kindly responds, "Of course!" and scoots close to the window in our two-seated row.

"We have three hours until our next stop guys so if you need to use the bathroom, use it now," our leader shouts over the intercom.

Three hours with three people in one row? My ass is going to suffocate in this journey.

"So, you say you like chocolate?" he asks. My eyes instantly light up.

"Am I human?" I respond.

"I hope so," he answers as he takes out two of my favorite Israeli chocolate bars from his backpack. He hands Jilly one and me the other.

"We can share, yes?" he asks.

"You can use this as payment for sitting here." I smile as I open the wrapper. Oh my god, caramel in the center. "I now forgive you for the emotional distress you caused me today. If you do it again, just have more chocolate nearby and we'll be fine." I confirm.

"Is this the way to your heart? I will keep that in mind," he smirks.

"It's like a knock at the entrance. It doesn't mean the door will open. Don't get too excited," I tease.

Mr. GQ asks us a lot of questions about our lives back home and the kinds of jobs we have at our age. Jilly is working for an advertising agency, and I am an event planner for a medical education company, which sound ridiculous in comparison to his line of work. He is a Commander in the Navy responsible for manning a ship of fourteen adolescent soldiers. At the young age of twenty-three, he had led his eighteen-year-old warriors from recent graduates to military men.

We talk for an hour, and the more I learn about him, the fonder I become. My heart rate starts to normalize. He no longer felt untouchable. The three of us simultaneously fall asleep during the ride and his hand falls on my thigh. Whether consciously or not, I choose not to move it. The day continues and he seems to have attached himself to me for every prolonged activity. Returning back to the bus, he continues to squeeze in our row after Jilly and I slid beside each other. I don't mind it as much this time.

I still can't quite understand why, out of all of the girls on the trip, he is gravitating towards me. I am not the skinniest, nor the tallest or the smallest. Why is he choosing to spend so much of his time with me? After donating my seat space with Jilly, sitting on my lap, alternating between the two of my legs, I ditch her for a new bus partner and Mr. GQ and I move to our own empty row in the back.

He chooses the window seat and I the aisle. He shifts his head facing mine and leans in where our eyes meet inches away, "So tell me, what does Brittany like to do?" he asks.

"Brittany likes to do a lot of things. I like to work out, tan, and eat." Oops. Should not have said eat, but I'm sure he realizes these thunder thighs didn't grow on their own.

"Not so successful with the tanning part, huh?" as he compares his skin next to mine.

No shit, compared to an Israeli, I'm basically a marshmallow. "My country has different sun rays than yours, so the temperature on your sun baking oven gives off more heat than mine."

"Is that so? You love comparing life to food," he mentions.

"Because what is life without food?" I ask.

"Death," he answers.

"Exactly." I assure.

"Do you have any brothers or sisters?" he asks.

"Yes, I have one older brother. He is amazing and is the human size version of the hulk." He asks me to show him my family. I pull up some pictures and he asks me about each member, then moving on to my closest friends. I'm stunned that he cares so much about people he will never meet.

He pulls out his cell phone to show me his parents, two older brothers, and nieces. He explains how his mother and grandparents are originally from England and moved to Israel after the Second World War. We talk the entire way to the hotel until it is time to leave the bus for the night.

We settle into our rooms and prepare for dinner. I take a seat with my girlfriends and the combination of delusion and exhaustion kicks in. I stare at my plate, feeling so thankful for my warm pita, spicy hummus, and mountain of Israeli salad. I noticed his absence at the start of dinner but did not notice his late entry, until I feel a hand slowly caresses my back. Without breaking my stare, he takes a seat at the table across from ours, more specifically, directly across from me. I was never good at the "sexy stare". That was my friend Yves's forte back home. So, I sink down and hide behind Jilly. Trying to finish my dinner, and yes, I *will* clean this plate, I catch him tilting his head to different sides to meet my eyes again. As flattered as I am, I don't play this game so I lean back again, slouch a little more, and place my knee against the table to make room for my food baby.

Within these organizational trips come organizational activities that require mandatory participation from our group. But outside, in the desert heat, is not the most ideal setting for activities post dinner and shower. The majority of us appear in sweatpants and sleep shirts until we find out we are playing capture the flag with water balloons as ammunition. Really? Adults don't play capture the flag. Feeling the moisture release from my pores, approaching the material of my sweatpants, I decide to sneak away to change. I am not taking a second shower in the hotel pocket sized, non-ventilated box, to sweat more on my current sweatiness.

I inconspicuously speed walk to the stairwell to change into shorts and spray a few sprits of perfume before returning to the battlefield. As I walk down the steps, he appears in my path wearing a green army training uniform and puts his hands on my shoulders.

"Kol b'sedar?" (*Is everything okay?*) He asks.

"Yes, I just had to change into shorts. I was hot," I respond.

His eyes scan my body and he kisses the top of my head, "Yes you are. I'll see you in a bit. Don't judge me for the behavior you're about to see, but I think you will enjoy it," he claims as he walks into the lobby.

I stop dead in my tracks. Did he just kiss my forehead? Heart attack in full swing. That man could wear a garbage bag and would still be miraculously beautiful. Two uniforms in one day is way too much for my heart rate to handle.

We stand in a circle around the soldiers until Mr. GQ races down the steps carrying bags filled with water balloons. Silence covers a two-minute period while the Pilot and Commander walk the outer line, checking our form to make sure it mirrors their military positions. I hear slow footsteps approaching when I feel a hand stroke my lower back. I flinch in surprise and he lets out a small laugh while continuing to pace. Once they reenter the circle, the soldiers disperse in all directions shouting at our faces in Hebrew. Don't they know none of us can understand a single word they're saying? This intimidation factor is not going to work well with this immature group of adults. Some of us burst into laughter. The boys run in circles for the soldiers to catch them and Jilly accidently sneezes in one of their faces. This is all very disorganized. One of the female soldiers blows her whistle and they return to the bags like a small army, tearing open the sides and pelting us with water balloons. Watching in another slow motion display (cue slow ballet background music) water soaking perfectly straightened hair, transparent backsides of white t-shirts, sandals flying in the air mid sprint, I quickly conclude that this shit is not for me. It's water, after all. I run into the trees at a pace I didn't know is humanly possible for my stature. Reassuring my list of dislikes there are two things I can add: unexpectedly sweating at night and getting wet from forces of nature other than God.

After finding 85% of our group visibly drenched and hiding for cover, the soldiers relent and the game is terminated. Jilly and I retreat to a corner of the lobby and FaceTime her parents. It wasn't until his face appeared in the screen of her phone that I realize he had been hovering behind us. He introduces himself to her parents and her mom admits that he is stunningly handsome. Ugh. We know. He offers me a cup of water and asks if he can pull me aside, sparking up more conversation on the couch. It is close to midnight and everyone makes their way up to their rooms when he grabs my arm and asks me to stay.

I hesitate, no – you have that look in your eye and that look historically leads to trouble. And the qualms of life start rolling in… I just met you this morning… I know what you're thinking… and as cute as you are… I'm not going there. This is the same reason I choose not to download dating apps because I'm afraid of strangers and awkward conversations. Also, the one time I did go on a dating app date, the guy ended up being gay so, never again.

My backup plans for these scenarios are to, of course, play dumb and pretend not to notice. "I'm really tired. Jet lag is hitting me. This place feels haunted. No thanks, I'm out."

"Well if you change your mind, here is my number," he adds to my phone.

I lie awake picking petals off of my invisible rose, revising Shakespeare: to hook up with him or to not hook up with him. That is most certainly the question. The real me would never give the kid a chance this early on in the game. However, since there is a time crunch on this short visitation, and he is the most beautiful man in the world, I decide to think of what I would *not* normally do. I would not normally consider hooking up with him so maybe I should consider it. Not tonight, but maybe like, tomorrow night.

"Hook Up" definition for all the mothers and Grandma Edith out there is just a kiss. Not a home run on the field if you know what I mean. There is always this unspoken question, to kiss or not to kiss on the first date? To go further or not go further on the third date? When is the acceptable time to pass the bases or bring it on home (not literally, but maybe literally if he's Zeus)? If I knew I only had a few short days with him, does that speed up the process of intimacy? The final decision would be my choice, but which "me" would make that decision? The "me" who would never take her foot off the brake because I have certain sets of standards and rules for myself, even though I am high level spellbound by his model-like beauty. Or the side of "me" I have never tapped into who goes full throttle through a stop sign thinking, I give zero fucks and I'm goin' in!

In this scenario, time will not tell. Therefore, fuck time.

I arise before my two roommates and step onto the balcony to watch the sun peek over Lake Kinneret. The only sound I hear is pure silence and the only thing I feel is pure bliss. Today we will visit a city that promises to make you feel magic in the air, beneath the walls, where chills form on the surface of your skin. If Dorothy were Jewish, a click of her heels would have landed her in Tzfat.

On our agenda is a visit to a Mikveh, where we would learn not only about its significance in the Jewish religion but also about how it innately holds significance in your life. A Mikveh, in non-formal terms, is a bath or body of water in which you would ritually immerse yourself as a form of both internal and external cleansing. The fluidity of words our

Mikveh educator, Talia, uses to explain the importance behind this action becomes magic for me that would last throughout the trip.

Talia grew up in Canada as a reform Jew and secured a career as a professional ballerina. At a show in New York, she met her musician husband, who she fell in love with just after one date. Neither he nor she were religious, but after consecrating their marriage way before they wed, they decided to visit Israel. Upon visiting the mystical spirit of the city Tzfat, their self-purpose awakened, and after that day, they chose to never leave. Approximately nine children later, here she is, sharing the Mikveh's purposefulness so powerfully, she had me convinced to join the pool party.

She never thought she would live her life any other way than she did in Canada. She was always open-minded but never stepped away from knowing and doing whatever she pleased. Her ballerina era mentality reminded me of myself at the age I am now. For her to transform her entire life after meeting the man of her dreams, visiting the land where she felt an instant connection, she claims she never felt a reason to look back on the life she had because the life she has now fulfilled her entirely. Listening to her, I sit wondering, if that opportunity knocked on my front door, would I notice? Would I be able to completely give up my life for another? Would I see it as giving up, or would I see it as sharing my life with another, selflessly? I wonder if my heart would be able to choose that over my mind.

This place holds a lot of memories for me. I have been here before. Mr. GQ remains by my side as we wander off to different parts of the city I've never seen. He is a born leader. I can see why his title suits him. I am so accustomed to being in control, but I like allowing him to lead me, for a change. How he passionately recollects historic tales upon these ancient grounds lights up my fire. Trailing the smell of seasoned lamb while we turn the corner, we fall upon the second-best part of the day, lunch. He offers to order for me, choosing two giant lafa sandwiches filled with lamb, cabbage, olives, salad, tahini, hummus and secret sauce. Heated up with a side of spicy because we always need a dash of spice in our lives.

We find a quiet space in a narrow stairway, looking out at the view of the city while lying against the cold steps. He places my legs over his and wipes the tahini dripping from my lips. That's love. He talks about some of his favorite foods and how tasting each present bite is like having an intimate affair with cuisine. "You don't want to go too slow and you don't want to go too fast. You want to enjoy each taste and smell because then it's all gone and you'll miss it," he says.

"And that's when you buy a second round," I add.

"I don't get the luxury of seconds out on the water. You get what you get and have to be happy with it. Slim pickings as you would say," he jokes.

"Do you ever fish off the boat and have a feast with the team?" I ask.

"No," he laughs, "but I've definitely thought about it and that would be a great idea."

"Not as good as this though," I indulge in my last bite.

"No. Never as good as this," he kisses my cheek.

We walk through the slim alleyways and pass the jewelry store where I bought matching rings with my mother. Where I bought my first car mezuzah when I was sixteen that still sits upon my dashboard. Where I purchased my first mezuzah for my apartment in college. So many memories on this street, all, of course, involving shopping. This time, I buy a rose colored, druzy necklace to continue my buying tradition. I would not change my ritual for the world. Standing in the store, he spots a necklace, studying it between his fingertips.

"Try it on," I suggest.

"No. I just think it's nice, but I don't need it," he puts it back.

"We don't need a lot of things but it's okay to want them." I place my hand beneath his collar noticing his neck is bare. "If it looks good and it feels good, and the price is right, we should do it. Plus, Jews always wear necklaces and you don't have one. I sense a problem, and a potential solution," I tease.

"This is why you're good at shopping, eh?" he recognizes.

"Sometimes we are allowed to treat ourselves. That's why we work hard," I affirm.

I clasp the necklace around his neck. The silver pendant of the state of Israel hangs off the base of his chest. The owner recommends the option to customize each side with whatever markings he likes.

"What should I put?" he asks.

"What's calling to you?" I question.

He looks at the sheet of designs and chooses the Star of David. "Is this good?" he asks.

"It's great," I agree. We hackle the owner to give us the best price and he agrees, so as long as we return together one day.

"I can't promise that but I can promise you he will wear this very well," I assure.

Prior to sundown, we finish the day in the holiest city of all, Jerusalem. To me, Tzfat is a city of magic and Jerusalem is a city of miracles. In Tzfat, I happen to shop. In Jerusalem, I happen to feel alive. All in all, these cities bring me gifts whether in the form of jewelry or spirit. To me, it's tradition.

We arrive at a new hotel where we will spend the weekend for Shabbat (*a day of rest in Jewish culture*). My favorite part of Shabbat in this city is visiting The Kotel (*also known as the Western Wall*). Upon arrival to the gates you can hear the cheerful hymns sounding from beyond the stone. Rushing inside we give Tzedakah (*donations*) and grab handfuls of red kabbalah strings to stuff into our bags. We all do it. We continue to push our way inside and when we arrive, there it is. The lights beaming bright onto the magnified stone, creases filled with greenery and handwritten notes from all over the world, to be blessed and tucked away to reach the other side. Wherever that other side is (we don't talk about it) but we believe in it. And that's what religion is all about, right? Believing in something.

Standing in front of this magnificent manifestation of history is one of the most spiritual experiences in any culture. The area is filled with joyous expressions, laughter, psalms, and life. It is where the true meaning of lechaim comes to form. Jilly, myself, and the girls from our group split sides walking to our section and the men to theirs. A stranger takes my hand as I hold on to the string of the others, forming a circle of women, singing, dancing and enjoying this universal language we refer to as life. Although we are strangers, we share a common bond of love and Jewish heritage, fueled by the spirit of Shabbat.

After building an appetite from the power of this service, we begin to walk back to the hotel for dinner.

Mr. GQ and I stroll down the quiet streets, reliving his memories through these neighborhoods. I'm tucked beneath his arm until he lowers his hand to meet mine. We are ahead of our group and decide to stop on the sidewalk to wait for the rest to catch up. He pulls a braided bracelet from his pocket and asks if I will tie it around his wrist. I ask where he got it from and he says a little boy sitting alone on the steps made it for him, after asking to sit beside him. I wrap it around his wrist with pleasure, tying a few knots until the last one is secure before raising my eyes to meet his, inches away from mine. He turns into me and my breathing stops. He tucks the hair behind my ear until the moment halts when Jilly spooks me from behind, shaking my shoulders and nearly scaring the shit out of me. The perfect moment interrupted by the remainder of the squad.

He pulls me to my feet to continue walking and all I can think about is what it would be like to kiss him. I would have liked for him to kiss me. It's only been a short time, but I can already sense an attachment growing towards him. I don't know what to make of it. This connection, which has never flamed so quickly, burns inside of me. I wonder if it is him or the essence of this night. Either way I look forward to the moment we explore closeness once again.

Romantically, our stomachs growl in unison as we approach the feast that awaits us. I've been looking forward to this festivity, as Shabbat includes a large spread and excessive amounts of wine because God told us to rest and drinking helps us rest, naturally.

If we were going to catch cabin fever in this hotel for two days, one thing we all agreed on is that we needed to find more wine. We had a lot of resting to do, you know? An hour walk feels really long in the desert.

As we bless it up and work on our scheme, I look back near the kitchen door and spot two loaves of challah and three bottles of wine, stacked next to the silverware. It is the challah I really want, but everyone else wants wine so I have to take one for the team. As inconspicuous as I can be, I make my way to the buffet, grabbing a plate while carefully loading pieces of challah, for me first. This is going to be a win-win situation here. I slowly gaze over the food to end up at the kitchen door while scouting out the area for waiters who might be watching. I grab a bottle of wine, wrap it in the length of my maxi dress and sprint back to our table, almost dropping my plate. Sitting down, I feel like I just won the gold metal of speed walking in the Olympics. The squad is thrilled.

Dinner turns into a party and the group disperses to different areas of the hotel. We are basically the only people staying in this converted frat house, so we took over the building pretty quickly. People go back to their rooms to drink the alcohol they smuggled in. Others hang around the lobby bar, a small counter with borderline transparent, cheap, plastic cups that I could crush easily with one finger. My friends walk outside on the patio to listen to music and smoke hookah with the Israelis. I join them but can't find the one Israeli that mattered to me. Where the hell did this kid go?

Walking to the bathroom, I bump into three boys.

"Where were you guys?" I ask.

"Playing truth or dare in our room. It got lame so we left. Is everyone outside?" they ask.

"Yes, through those doors," I point, "Who's up there?" I ask.

They named about ten people. How they even fit in that shoebox of a room is beyond me, but most importantly the last name was the one that stuck. I scan the people descending from the stairs in a rush to the bar when I realize, two faces have not appeared.

"Who's up there now?" My final question.

One answered. Mr. GQ and another girl. Tisk fucking tisk.

Pushing the bathroom door like it's my worst fucking enemy, I grab the base of the sink with all of my might. Looking into the mirror my mind goes wild. Why is this bothering me? Do I have a right to care? I know I just met him, but I feel like I've been played. Why would he spend days pursuing me in the first place and now is looking elsewhere, because we haven't kissed? I don't fucking think so.

I walk back to the patio to find Jilly. I replay in my head, "Am I crazy? No. Am I intoxicated? Eh. Do I need more wine? Yes. Do I hate him? YES!"

Before I make it outside, half of the group returns inside the lobby. I decide to join them. As we pour more wine and our circle expands, I hear a shout from the elevators. Our heads turn and a girl walks into the foyer tying her hair up as Mr. GQ follows behind, noticeably tucking in his shirt. I rub my eyes, feeling sick to my stomach. He runs over, giving high fives to our seated circle, like an unattractive, five-year-old drunk, when he positions himself in front of me, waiting for a reaction. I turn my head to face the window.

"No love?" he asks. "Fine." He pulls up a chair and pushes mine over to make room. I don't move. He sits down beside me staring with a dedicated gaze. Maintaining my eye contact with the window, I cross one leg over the other and rest back in my chair.

"What?" I ask.

He points his drunken finger to me, "You're not like other girls."

I roll my eyes, "I know I'm not." Ugh, what is he even SAYING.

"There is something about you. I knew it from the first… that is very special… you are very special," he mutters.

"I know I am," I reclaim.

"No really, you are," he points.

"Trust me, I know!" I respond.

He fixates his gaze and attempts to touch my arm. I smack it away.

"Why are you acting this way? What happened?" he asks.

"Because you are like all the other guys I know and, unlike your feelings, I don't find you special at all," I answer.

"Yeah?" he asks. "I can change that." He grabs hold of my chair, scooping me from underneath and throwing me over his shoulder in one quick drive. What the fuck is this guy doing. Looking upside down with my arm pleadingly outstretched, I scream for Jilly, but he makes his way to a couch in the back. I kick and try to wiggle out of his hold until I accidently cocoon myself in my dress, losing freedom of all lower movement. He sits me down in a chair but I quickly escape, only to make it to the chair across from him where he catches me.

"No escaping," he commands.

Sigh. I cross my arms.

He leans forward. "Why are you upset with me?"

"You know why," I lean in, "I know everything." I look away. He maneuvers his feet around the leg of my chair and pulls me around the table until I'm beside him.

"I'm sorry. Please forgive me," he pleads, "It was stupid. I will not let you go. There is something about you I… I just feel like I know you. You're special to me. Look at me... please. I can't handle you being upset. Let me fix it."

I try to push away and he strengthens his hold. I know that I don't have the right to be angry, but somewhere deep inside I feel that I do.

"You just met me! You don't even know me. How can I be so special to you when you intentionally make out with another girl after trying to kiss me two hours ago? Sorry Charlie, I do not share saliva with other women. You made your bed now you have to lie in it." I see Jilly walking by and I yell for her to come save me. She stops, smiles, and waves her hand as she makes her way outside.

"Who's Charlie? What bed?" he responds. I forgot he's from another country.

"It's a saying! Ugh, let me go! I'm done with you."

I ascend from my seat when he lifts me out of my chair onto his lap.

"Jesus, do you have super human strength? I don't get it!"

I try to wiggle out of his arm lock and again, I lose. I tell him if he lets go I promise to calm down and sit in place. He does, and so do I, as I think of an escape plan.

"Can we have an honest conversation?" he asks.

"I don't know if you can handle an honest conversation, but sure," I answer.

"From the first time I saw you on the bus, the first thing I noticed was your smile. And your laugh. Everyone kind of looked the same and for some reason my vision narrowed to you. And then I passed by and you looked away and I thought okay, I will go to the back of the bus. There will be time to talk to you later. Then later came. At the picnic table. In the water. Then back on the bus. I made sure I was going to sit next to you. So, I asked. You said yes, kind of. And that was it."

"Ok. What's your point?" I ask.

"It was a game. Everyone played along and so did I. It didn't mean anything. Even if you were in the room, I wouldn't have played with you because I would want this to be meaningful. You also don't seem like the type to play those games," he says.

"You're right. Because I hold value to myself and my self-worth. To some people, a kiss means nothing. To me, it means a lot more than nothing, and that's okay with me. I choose not to make out with someone in front of ten people in a confined space. Not my cup of tea, but you do you. Just don't try to get close to me anymore."

"No. This is not what I wanted!" he slams his hand on the table.

"Calm down. Let me explain something to you. I am not upset at the fact that you played this stupid game. You owe me absolutely nothing in this world. But I very much took a liking to you, being with you fifteen hours out of the day. You led me on and now you really disappointed me. The end."

"How can I make it up to you?" he asks.

"You can't. That ship has sailed. Your ship. Sailed." I wave, "Oh, there it is. Do you see it? Gone." He looks out in the distance. "You're an idiot."

For a second, he tries to kiss me. I slap him across the face. "Keep your saliva. I don't want it." I retract.

I slide between his legs under the table until he catches the end of my dress and slides me back through. This stupid dress is ruining my life. I lie on the floor.

"Wait!" I yell. "I surrender. I give up. I won't run." I state, out of breath.

He brings me to a standing position in front of him and holds up one finger.

"If you give me one hug, I promise to leave you alone for tonight. I can't say for tomorrow, but I will for tonight," he propositions.

I count in my head how many times I have already lost tonight and agree to his proposition. The moment he opens his wingspan, I make a run for the stairs.

Sitting on my squeaky, deflated twin mattress, I can't help feeling a pit in my stomach. He made me so angry. He made me believe that all guys aren't as bad as we think they are. That some good guys do exist, believe it or not. I believed it. Now, I do not. In reality, he owes me nothing. But because he showed me something, I can't reverse the thought of admiring him as much as I do. After only two days, a piece of my heart was broken that I could not explain and was embarrassed to admit.

Maybe that was it. I'm not jealous. I'm embarrassed. I am embarrassed that I gave him my time and attention and that I was going to give him a chance, which is something I never do. I felt betrayed. The betrayal turned into embarrassment, and now I just feel ashamed. I realized two factors this evening. That he is actually human and I guess so am I. That I do have a heart that bleeds, even though I thought feelings didn't really exist inside me. With him, feelings only existed, and I want that emotional power back. I wish I could blame this on PMS, but it's not that time of the month, so I firmly blame him for making me mental. What I don't blame him for is for making me feel. For making me feel what it's like to have strong unintended feelings so quickly, for what feels like the first time. But he is not forgiven, because as I get ready for bed and turn over my brick solid pillow, I have only one real feeling in the back of my mind…

and that's a big fuck you.

(Lights out)

Saturday

I close my eyes, bringing my knees into my chest as I sink to the bottom of the pool, the only body of water I can handle. The water feels cool on my skin and I can feel the bubbles freeing from my nostrils as I breathe out. How long can I hold my breath in this deep end? I begin to hear a sound coming from above, of something familiar but cannot make out the words. It's getting louder and louder. It sounds like music. I push my feet off of the floor, aiming for the surface until I wake up. Oh, it's just John Newman and my alarm. I look at the time. 8:00 AM. Are you kidding me? Why did I set an alarm for this early? Then I remember. Last night in my drunken state, I convinced Liza, the part-time yoga instructor, to teach a morning class. Bad idea. I shake Jilly and our roommate Dana to join me. In idle motion, shockingly they do and we prepare for bending and breakfast.

Eleven of us show up and find a small empty room downstairs. I detect scents of mold mixed with haunted house aromas but for this purpose, it will do. We stack the chairs against the walls before laying our towels down as mats. As I spread out my towel behind Jilly's, a shadow casts over me. I look up and see a hungover, smiling, tan presence in tiny black shorts. As much as I hate him, I can't help but laugh.

"Are you European now?" I ask.

"European? These are my gym shorts. You don't like them?" he smiles.

"I mean... they show a lot for these... types of poses," I acknowledge.

"I can move very well in them. Just wait and see," he says.

"I'll wait and see over here. You wait and see over there next to your girlfriend, in the front," I point.

"No, I told you. You and me," he signals.

"You and me nothing," I stretch out my towel trying to take up more space than its size would allow.

He turns away from me, "Alex, is this place taken?"

"Yes, it is," I respond for him.

"No, are you Alex? I didn't think so," he says.

He pulls my towel from under me to make room for his. We start out in Sukhasana and I feel him touching my thigh with the back of his hand.

"Stop it," I whisper, "You do not exist to me," I place my sunglasses over my eyes so we cannot make eye contact.

In tree pose, he starts to poke my sides so that I lose balance and fall over. Attempting to keep my shades from sliding off my face, I am determined to stand my ground, even while on one leg. I ask Jilly to switch with me and she waves me off in refusal. Each time we transition to the opposite position he faces me instead, winking while he twists his body.

"You are the worst," I whisper, as he tries to hold my hand between transitions.

"I'm gunna make you love me, love me, say that you love me," he whispers, "Know that song?" he asks while raising his eyebrows.

"Yes I do – shh," this kid is crazy.

"That's our song now," he smiles.

"Shh, no. We don't have a song," I answer.

Minutes pass and he finally leaves me alone. I can't help but notice how impressively flexible he is. Doesn't matter anyway. We end the class with meditation and the lights turn off as the music enhances. She repeats a mantra and he takes hold of my hand in the dark. At first, I flinch to pull away and he holds the grip even tighter.

"Just enjoy it. I'm stronger than you anyway," he whispers.

I exhale deeply while shaking my head. I ask the universe for guidance, and forgiveness, on how to allow myself to give in to this man. Despite the darkness, I feel his stare. With his grip still in mine, his hands feel distinctively soft for a man. Even though I feel that he doesn't deserve my affection, I decide not to fight it, but to allow it. My hand feels comfort in his while I try to use this time to internally release my bitterness. The lights turn back on and we gather applause for our fellow group participant leading a successful class. As I stand up to fold my towel, he grabs my wrist, "Namaste princess, do you forgive me?" he asks. Although it is easier to hate him, something inside me doesn't want to. I don't know if it was this yoga session or my unrested sleep, but I have no more energy to waste on resenting him. I wave off, "Fine." I carry my towel and make my way up the stairs, following the scent of breakfast.

He follows behind and sits at the other side of the table. After inhaling the buffet of food, I can't help but feel like my food baby and I could use a nap. Jilly agrees and we decide to gather some fruit before returning upstairs. As I rise from my chair, Mr. GQ bends down to my ear and asks if we could talk later. I tell him I would think about it and return to my room. Jilly and I sit on the beds and I finally tell her everything that happened the night before. I ask her why my heart was hurting and why I was feeling so rebellious towards him. She convinces me that this is what girls do, and maybe he has an effect on me that no one else has had before. Fortunately, I'm not as crazy as I thought. The whole female population is, and with that universal diagnosis, I can sleep soundly.

We wake up in time for a mandatory group activity in the lobby. I skim the room and notice Mr. GQ is absent. When he arrives at lunch, his eyes flicker past me and I think he is respecting my decision to part. Keeping his distance three-table lengths from me, I start to wind down and the lunchroom empties out.

I'm happily picking apart my no-guilt chocolate rugelach as the chair pulls out from under my crossed, rested legs.

"Is this seat taken?" he asks.

"I don't know. Out of all 250 chairs in this room this is the only chair you want to sit in?" he crosses my ankles and places them atop his knee.

"Yes, now we both win," he smiles.

I squint, "He-he so funny. What do you want?"

"I want to talk to you," he says.

"Talk," I continue.

"No, I want to talk to you alone. Can we go somewhere quiet?" he asks.

I look at Jilly and she looks back, "I'm not getting involved," as she removes herself from the table. Thanks a lot Jill.

He strokes my leg, "Very smooth," he notices.

"Lucky for you, if you tried that this time yesterday, it would have been a different texture, that's for sure."

"I wouldn't mind. I've probably seen worse," he lifts up his leg exposing his shin, "no competition here sweetheart. This is golden hair."

Forgetting my earlier resilience, I burst into laughter.

"Come, I want to show you something," he offers his hand.

Walking out of the meal room, I realize that it's much more difficult to fight him, than not. Even though he gives me a mixed feeling of ease and fire, a part of me wants to break through the existing pit in my stomach and give him a chance. I don't want to care about what happened last night. I want to go back to discovering his charm as I did before. But will my mind be able to let me cross that barrier?

Walking to the floor of his room, my heart picks up its pace and I struggle to define and separate my feelings. Rebellious against my wits, but nervous? Anxious that I am walking into a mistake but exhilarated that I am consciously making one? I want to deny all thoughts and get my mind out of the driver's seat. I want to be the passenger, and let the moment happen naturally, without this mental rollercoaster.

Stepping into the corridor, we notice a few rooms across the way with the doors cracked open. Abandoned paint cans and brushes left at the end of the hall. No workers in sight. We walk to the second door and he knocks, "Hello? Anyone home?"

He slowly opens the door and steps inside. He signals me in, "Are you coming?"

"I feel like we aren't supposed to be here," I whisper.

"Isn't that the fun of it?" he asks.

He pulls me in and closes the door behind. The room smells like a fresh coat of wet paint. In between the white walls, a large window exposes the birds on the trees. He rolls onto the bed and searches for music on his phone. He asks what music I like to listen to, but I don't answer, assuming he wouldn't have heard of it anyway. I ask him to surprise me with his one of his favorites. Shockingly, he picks one of mine, Kygo. He raises his hands in the air singing the lyrics, clearly craving his time to shine, which calms the undeniable tension. I stand next to the wall with my foot propped up until I realize the stencil of my sneaker indented the wet paint. Fack.

"I won't bite today, just come sit with me," he says.

A slower song comes on and he reaches out to take my hand, "If not that, will you have this dance with me?" he asks. My eyes answer yes.

He pulls me in close, swaying me from side to side, scooping me into the air until our noses slightly touch. I can't help but match his smile and laugh at this mini private concert he created in this serene abode. He lays a kiss on my cheek and spins me out, to then bow and thank the imaginary audience for watching our debut.

He falls upon the bed and stacks pillows to lean against. "Aren't I a great dancer?" he asks.

"You're alright. I'd give you a 9 out of 10," I respond.

"A 9 out of 10! Wow, you are a tough judge," he answers. "What would have given me a perfect score?"

"A dip… at the end," I assure.

"A dip? Ohh you're right that would have been a good move," he agrees.

"Great move. Maybe next time," I glimmer.

"What if I have a better move?" he asks.

"What would that be?" I ask.

I rest back on my hands diagonally from him as he unties my shoelaces. One by one, he gradually slips off my shoes placing each on the floor alongside his. "Comfortable?" he asks.

I nod not breaking his stare. Studying his oceanic blue eyes, I can't help but notice the symmetrical beauty illumining off his face.

He pats the spot adjacent to him. I crawl over and support my head on the pillow. I lean in close, "Is this your move?"

He tucks my hair behind my ear and traces the skin underneath my chin, "No," he answers, "this is." He pulls me closer and I place my finger upon his lips.

"If I'm so special… I deserve a brand-new move," I command.

I can't help but snicker. His eyes seem up for the challenge.

"How about I tell you the story of my first move?" he asks. He tells me about his first kiss at the age of fifteen. He went on a camping trip with his friends nearby a lake. One of the girls on the trip was someone he liked. Since they were friends first, he didn't know how to relay his feelings and thought this trip would be the perfect opportunity to do so. He asked her if she wanted to watch the sunset, near the rocks by the lagoon. She said yes, and they climbed on top of a rock to get a better view through the trees. He grabbed her arm to help her up but they both fall back into the water. All hopes of romanticism vanished. Until on shore, where they air-dried on the grass he stole his first kiss and his infamous "move" was born.

"Is that what you tried to do with me in the Jordan River because that was a major fail," I tease.

He laughs. "Honestly it wasn't, but what if it was? What move works for you?"

"Hmm…I don't think there's a specific move. Honestly, guys usually ask for permission first. *That's* how special I am," I amuse.

"So, once they ask you for permission, you say yes?" he asks.

"Not always. I'm like the prey in the woods you wait the entire day to hunt, and you either catch me, or you don't."

"But if he asks permission then you know it's coming and there's the option you can say no. Where's the thrill in that?" he asks.

I've never thought about it that way. "Good point."

"I would rather take you by surprise so that you don't have time to hesitate," he says, "Therefore, I will wait."

His phone pings and he mentions he's expected to meet the soldiers in the lobby. I don't want our time to end, but I walk ahead of him anyway. As I cautiously open the door, he stops me, placing his hand against the wood, turning my body to face his. Wrapping his arm around my waist, he lowers his eyes to mine and shifts his gaze to my lips. Slowly, he leans in and firmly plants a kiss. "A man never waits too long for his prey. He catches it when she least expects it," he whispers. I feel like a girl being kissed by a man for the first time. He closes the door.

The First Kiss

He picks me up against his chest and lays me softly onto the bed. Slowly lowering his body on top of mine, my heart races. His lips are warm and hands are soft as he gently interlaces my palm into his. For what seems like hours we lay in silence as he explores my features.

I take in this moment of innocence. Hours pass as we lie beside each other through deep conversation. We begin to drift asleep. He asks if I will stay and I choose to comply. I embrace his fit against mine as he respects the line between us. He locks his arm beneath my own while interweaving our hands as one. The scent of his cologne charms me to dream where I never thought I'd be, in this fantasy-reality.

I can't recall the last time I laid next to a man who was content with just feeling the warmth radiate off a woman's body. Who was satisfied with the comfort of a woman's embrace and nothing more. The most innocent love I experienced up to now was in high school. We were young, we grew to love, and it was pure, paced, and easy. But at this age, it's rare to find another who can be fulfilled by only a harmless kiss. What I've noticed this time with Mr. GQ, is that there was no expectation. With other guys, there is always an expectation. Even if it is not verbally discussed, it exists by nature. He wanted nothing more than to just coexist. And I wanted to exist, with him.

I think back to the guys I've previously been involved with and realize I was never able to truly be myself. Some guys were too polished, too poised, too mature, or too immature. I always felt as if I were settling or wasting my time, convincing myself to develop feelings when I knew there weren't any. This time I wasn't settling. I am perfectly sure of my feelings and what I want to do with them.

I turn over to face him. His eyes open softly. He nestles his head into my chest bringing me in closer. His breath is soft on my neck as our hearts beat in unison. This quiet closeness feels so normal and I start to understand why I haven't felt this way before. Lying next to him, I realize it wasn't the expectation, but the reality of feeling as if I had known him my entire life. That my connection with him allowed me to expose my true, most authentic self. I didn't care to be filtered, to hurt his feelings, or to not be honest with my vocal thoughts. Something within him admires that about me, despite the fact that we hardly know each other. He doesn't feel like a stranger to me. It feels like he is already mine.

His phone vibrates on the nightstand, stirring us from our dreamlike state. I squint at the time, realizing we only have an hour before we have to leave for dinner.

"Shit! I have to go. I only have an hour to get ready."

"Wait. Don't leave just yet," he insists.

I shimmy off the bed when he grips me closer.

"One more kiss?" he charms.

"One kiss," I lean in and absorb the feeling of his soft lips on mine.

"Let me walk you out at least."

"Oh yeah? Are you going to give me door to door service?" I tease.

"Of course I am. Because you're special."

He peeks out the door and sees no one in sight. "It is clear," he winks. He lifts me onto his back and runs up the stairs to my room. I thank him for his five-star service and he pulls me in, cradling my face in his hands. He leans in for another kiss and pecks both my cheeks before walking away. I slide in my room key to unlock the door when he turns back to shout, "I'll pick you up at eight!" then disappears into the stairwell.

Jilly and Dana peep their heads as I walk in the door, "Hello lady! Where have you been?" they ask. I feel the heat rise to my cheeks but keep the days' activities to myself before stepping into the shower. I relish in this newfound giddiness and permanent smile from today's adventure. Feeling like a teenager on her first date, I can't help but wait for what's in store tonight.

8:00 PM sharp, there is melodic knock on the door. I turn the knob to find his *cool* presence leaning against the frame. He directs his toothpick pointing to my chest.

"Where is the rest of your shirt?" he asks.

"On my body," I answer.

He points to the extreme low cut of my blouse and glares. "I disagree. Change. I'll wait."

"Sorry dad, you're lucky I'm even wearing clothes. It's a desert storm in here. You try getting ready with three girls and constant steam from the shower."

He tries to close the opening of my blouse but fails as the seams are taped to my chest. "You can put this on," he tosses his sweater over my ribcage.

"In this room you are not the Commander. Stop acting like one," I throw the sweater back in his face.

I pick up my stride as I head to the elevator and he lifts me into his arms. "I'll show you who's in charge," he commands.

"Jesus! You do have super human strength."

The elevator door opens and he places me atop the railings. Cornering my body against the wall, he grabs the sides of my thighs placing his mouth upon mine. The doors reopen at the lobby and as he walks out, I stand, spent. *Jesus Criest*. I fix my hair. He looks back laughing and grabs my hand leading us to the bus.

He slides me into the seat, resting my legs across his lap. As the engine starts, the lights dim and radio turns on. The group shouts and sings to the music when his palm grips behind my neck and he advances for a kiss.

"Woah, woah, what are you doing?" I ask.

"What do you mean? What's wrong?" he questions. "Ohh, do you not like PDA?" he asks, realizing that the rows in front, next to, and behind are all watching us, waiting for his next move. I'm shocked he even knows what PDA means. "No, I don't," I answer.

He starts to laugh. "Why not? You don't want to show how much you like me?" He kisses the sides of my neck. "Ehh one step at a time," I answer. "Seriously. You're making me nervous I don't like this kind of global attention," I plead. He leans back into his chair. "Fine. But know that move number two is in the making." Peering out the window, I notice I'm slipping back into my old ways. I was so used to being private about my personal life, I didn't like showing it to the world. But why do I even care? Realizing I will regret every chance I don't take with him, I throw my privacy out the window. Who fucking cares! Taking hold of his chin, I bring him in to kiss me. His hand embraces the sides of my thigh as the music gets louder. It feels like were alone once again. "It's just you and me. Don't worry about everyone else," he says, "And I like your shirt, but for my eyes only." With him singing songs in my ear, I drown in his affection as the bus reaches our destination.

We walk hand in hand through a strip of bars and restaurants that line Ben Yehuda Street. After settling on a restaurant that could accommodate a twenty-person table, we pass around large plates of foods, drinks, shots, and hookah. Enjoying the first part of the evening surrounded by beautiful Jerusalem stone and Israeli music, we leave in search of a club that would fit our capacity and play our kind of music.

Before we walk inside his lips graze my ear, "Do you trust me?" he whispers. "Should I?" I tease. "Follow me." He takes my arm and runs with me through an alley of bright colored umbrellas overhead. The narrow passageway leads us to two men standing in front of a red velvet rope. "Is this a secret club? I feel like I'm back in Miami," I joke. "Do you guys want to come inside?" they ask. I look at him. "Sure?" I respond. "Come on in." He opens the rope. That was too easy.

We walk down a hallway and the music gets louder with each step. He opens a curtain exposing a stairwell leading underground to a black painted room. Flashing lights and white smoke fill the space, as we look over the balcony to a dancing crowd below. We can feel the vibration from the music through our feet and make our way down to the dance floor. He turns me around and I get lost in his eyes while we dance. I have never been that girl to make out in the middle of the dance floor, but I am that girl tonight. I feel electric.

Lights moving. Floor pulsating. Music blaring. I feel the beats in my bloodline. Looking at him, no one else exists but us, and that's exactly how I want it. Heading over to the bar, he buys me a drink. We look at the time not realizing over an hour has already passed. Our bus leaves in fifteen minutes and we have to head back.

We haste out of the club and back through the umbrella-hanging street. He walks ahead of me trying to keep the dancing alive but I pause to air myself out. Our group walks out of a bar, and Jilly runs over, worried about where I've been. I hear Rihanna in the background and rap her lyrics to calm her anger about my absence.

On the ride home, our group makes a plan to continue the party when we get back. At the hotel, the boys grab a speaker and we continue our adult-mitzvah in the hotel's basement. With fifty people crammed into a small-unventilated space, things got heated fast. I step onto a chair by the nearest air vent. Girls will *always* find air vents when it's too hot for comfort. I look around and catch Mr. GQ's gaze in the corner of my eye. He posts up against the wall and signals me over. I descend from the chair, pushing through the compacted crowd until I reach him.

"Do you want to get out of here?" he asks. I don't hesitate and grab his hand. He leads me to a stairwell and we walk all the way up until we reach the rooftop. No matter how fit I think I may be, walking upstairs will always leave me out of breath.

He pushes open the door placing his shoe as a doorstopper to prevent being locked out. As bad as that predicament may sound, I actually wouldn't be mad if it happened. What a complete 180 from where we were last night. He lays his sweater down flat for me to sit and we fall softly back on the concrete. Feeling so fortunate for this cool breeze, the views are even better.

It's blissfully quiet. He takes my hand and we lay in silence while looking up at the endless night sky. I feel like I can see every star from up here with crystal clarity. Every time I've visited Israel, I happen to see a shooting star. May be hard to believe, but it's true. Just one of the many reasons I find this place so enchanting. We rest in stillness as he traces the outer form of my palm. Admiring his soulful face he smiles, and I gaze back up towards the sky. Tonight, I see two shooting stars traveling above but I don't ask him if he saw them.

8 years ago. My first journey to Israel was with a youth leadership organization. My high school boyfriend and I were in the same program and we traveled together on this trip. We spent four days camped out on a beach with our entire group. Each night, different members would be appointed to rotate as night watch duty while everyone slept. We were assigned together. As we were supposed to be carrying out this task, we snuck off, running towards the sand to sit atop red beach chairs, glaring up at the sky. No one was around. Just him and me. There is nothing as calming as the waves of the ocean and the darkness of a starry night. This was the first time I ever saw a shooting star. I never told my ex-boyfriend what I had witnessed as I felt this moment belonged to me. Normally when you experience this next to someone you "love" you would think about wishing to be with them forever, or something in that cliché department. But I didn't.

Maybe because I wasn't sure if I really loved my boyfriend at the time. Or maybe I was afraid to admit that I was convincing myself to love him, when my intuition told me I didn't. I do, though, remember what I wished for. I wished for happiness, success, and the power of knowing exactly what I wanted in life. Selfish? Maybe. But at fifteen this is what I wished for.

As I lay next to Mr. GQ, I think about my current situation in love, in my career and in life. The result leads to a self-confession. I'm not happy. And seeing this shooting star, I ask myself, what do I really want? What in my life can I change and what can I not? I'm not happy with my job. I'm not happy where I live. My love life is nonexistent, so where does that leave me now? Looking at him is the happiest I have been in a very long time. A happiness I didn't think I needed or wanted, but it fits, given the circumstances.

I can change my job. I can change where I live, but those changes are extreme and I don't take those types of risks. I am still in my first post-college job, I am still living in the city I was born, and as a result I've been carefully content. But shouldn't there be more to life than contentedness? I wanted more. But how do I get there?

Now, given a second chance at a shooting star, I am confident in knowing what to wish for. Happiness, direction, and love. For once, I know exactly what I want.

Mr. GQ turns to me and asks, "What are you thinking?"

I lay my head upon his chest, "A lot of things."

His lips mark the top of my head while he runs his fingers though my hair.

"How about you tell me a story," he asks. I smirk and tell him about the first time I saw a shooting star.

Sunday

Although I only slept five hours, I wake completely refreshed. Breakfast doesn't start for another hour, so I plan to sneak out of the room and go for a walk. I slide on my workout clothes and splash water on my face, a short routine knowing I will complete my seven-step face regimen when I return.

The lobby is empty. I push through the revolving hotel door into the parking lot. Slipping in my headphones, I press shuffle in my music library. A cool breeze brushes my skin and as the first song plays, I decide to run.

Running is not something I usually do. Sure, I've tried it. I've bought special shoes for it, but plain and simple, my body isn't a fan. Today, however, my body changed its mind. Running through a quiet and sleeping city is comforting. Fighting the breath uphill on the streets and narrow stoned sidewalks is easier than walking the flight of stairs to the roof. As I pass alleyways of houses with laundry drying overhead, flower boxes in balconies overflowing to the floor, I discover an unfamiliar wave of vitality. Running for thirty minutes I realize, I need to make a change in my life. Whether I feel prepared for it or not, I am ready to take a risk.

While the girls sleep, I take my precious time getting ready and reflect on how different this feels from my mornings back home. Whether it's heading to work, the gym or home, I am always in a rush, constantly battling the clock.

Not rushing feels great. Waking up early actually feels great, but waiting to eat is never great. The girls start to waken when starvation pains start to hit. I decide to head down without them so I can continue my morning thoughts. I head down the steps and find a familiar face zipping up his backpack two flights down. I sneak up behind him and place my hands over Mr. GQ's eyes. He arranges his hands over my ass.

"Hey!" I laugh. "Hmmm I wonder whose little hands these could be?" he coyly asks, removing my hands to kiss each of my wrists. We walk down to breakfast together, my fear of PDA gone, once and for all.

After finding a table where we can sit alone, we go our separate ways to the table buffets. Untouched scoops of hummus with fresh, red pepper outlined and oil seeping through, I am in heaven. I would never normally choose hummus for breakfast, but when I'm here, my taste buds convert. A scoop of this, and a scoop of that, my plate is sky high and so am I. Back at the table, Mr. GQ brings me chocolate and cheese filled pastries with a glass of freshly squeezed orange juice. It must have been the best orange juice I have ever tasted, and not just because he brought it for me.

"So, can we talk more about life?" he asks.

"We can," I interest.

"What are your plans for the future in the next couple of months?" he asks.

"Next couple of months? I'll be chained to a desk working. But next year I'll be twenty-five and I would love to move somewhere for a year. It's something I've always wanted to do, but I don't think it will ever happen. Why, do you have plans for me?" I amuse.

"I just might," he suggests, "I think you should do it. Move somewhere for a year. If you don't like it, you can always move back," he says.

"That's the thing... if I don't like it I *should* stay, because I'll never know what it's like to not live in my safe place. Unsafe, I may feel daring, spontaneous, rebellious, like I was when I decided to give you a chance."

"So rebellious, and how is that working out for you?" he asks.

"In this moment, pretty good! This orange juice is great thanks..." I wink as I finish drinking the glass.

"Are you ready to hear my suggestion?" he inquires.

"Dying to," I take a bite of the cheese Danish.

"Why don't you move to Israel?" he asks.

I choke. "Seriously?"

"Yes, seriously. Why would I not be serious?" he argues.

"And what would I do here?" I ask.

"You can hang out with me in Eilat and work on your much needed tan," he smiles, "I have a great pool so you won't drown in the ocean without my supervision. I know how you are with water."

My eyes widen. Is this a... *you're asking me to **move-in** to another country for you, after just meeting you* - question? Gulp. I never thought I would actually go through with relocating my life, even if I wanted to. That was just a hopeful, quarter-life goal of *mine*. Would I even consider this? Would I seriously move here and attempt running full-time with this Naval Dolce & Gabbana model? Would I be moving for me, or would I really be moving, for him?

"I was thinking more of like…London. I have a killer accent and I think I could blend in with my pale skin you know? But write me an offer I can't refuse and I'll look into my aspirations of being a professional tanner." I'm freaking out inside. "What about you? What's Mr. GQ's big five-year plan?" I ask.

"Well, I have six months left in the army and I decide whether to extend my position or try something new. I may go to architecture school or maybe go to the US to be in Friends of the IDF…maybe travel for a bit. I don't know yet," he answers.

Jilly and Dana join us at the table and our conversation comes to a halt. The girls tell us about the rest of their night and we accompany them while they eat. I can't help but be distracted by my conversation with Mr. GQ. Would he actually come to the states? Would I actually move here for him? Is this path to love worth leaving everything for, to try living a life, together?

Before making our way to the bus, I am completely unfocused. I pass a bowl of apples and my focus shifts. I put some in my bag since I can't be without snacks at all times. I hand some to my crew as well because when I'm in a state of hunger, sharing is not an option. Every human for themselves.

Mr. GQ leads us into a row and I nestle into his hold. I'm taken aback, once again, by how natural and effortless it is to be with him. I have never met another guy who I have felt more of a complete version of myself, and if that still wasn't enough, that he was an additional part of me. I can't believe I almost let my fear stop me from embracing this connection. I'm proud that I broke out of old habits to be able to merge with him. So much has changed in such a short time. I learned to not care too much and worry about what everyone else thinks. I think that was always my problem. Caring too much in all things in life. His love of my thighs (my appetite), my laugh, my smile, and my potential ADD moments, wrapped in a candy-sized frame was unlike anything I had known before. The way he holds my hand, places my hair to one side, and lifts me for a kiss. Because of him I knew, I wouldn't settle for anything less.

Over the course of the day, he does not leave my side and I do not leave his. I sense my body and awareness magnetize towards his every movement. When he's not by my side, I capture his stare, and feel his shadow nearby. He comes up behind me and holds me in close, placing his hands over my pulse. I want to keep him. And that is the part I don't know how to do.

We walk uphill and arrive at Hezekiah's tunnel in Jerusalem. This tunnel was carved thousands of years ago underneath the City of David and still exists today.

As we prepare to walk through the completely dark space, the water rises from my ankles to the tops of my thighs. Most tall people have to duck for the entire length of the way, but for short people like myself, this tunnel was perfect height. We sit in the waiting area slipping on our water shoes and retrieve small flashlights to guide our way through the tunnel. I didn't get a flashlight so Mr. GQ kindly offers to share his with me. I wonder if this was God's plan, or his?

One by one we walk into the tunnel. The water continues to ascent the deeper we tread, causing the hairs on my skin to rise with the water's cold temperature. I glide my hands across the cold crevices in the stone, feeling for the pathway ahead. In the distance I hear splashes and screams of pain from the tall community who don't see the dips in the ceilings. Poor guys. The majority of us without light, feeling our way through the darkness, come to a standstill. Mr. GQ turns off his light and closes in behind me. He places his hands on my body feeling the sides of my chest to my hips. Softly placing his lips down the side of my neck until they announce, "We're moving!" He steps back turning back on the light, which wasn't the only thing he turned on.

Each time we stop, Mr. GQ explores a different part of me and I let him. His body pressing against mine, I can feel his every muscle. I turn to face him to connect my body and lips to his. To feel and to taste, to smell and to hear his deep exhales in the dark.

Light starts to shine from the end of the tunnel, as he pulls me in for a final caress. Sight unseen all my senses aroused, I can't help but feel stunned by his effect on me. In such a short period of time, how could one person transform my sensations and perceptions? Is it lust? Or is this love? My head spins. I think it's love.

Walking down the steps approaching the Kot... already sense its energy running through me. My mo... run and thoughts of clarity have prepared me for this momen... of sanctity. I stand with my heart open, feeling the vibrational frequencies against my palms. Feeling at peace, I am ready to proceed forward and connect to my spiritual routes.

I center my palms on the cold stonewall and press my forehead against its surface. In the past I've brought a pre-written note to place into the crevice of the wall. I knew precisely what I wanted to say. This time, however, I chose to stand in stillness and feel the power of the wall's spirit run through me. Closing my eyes while opening my awareness, I breathe into my thoughts.

White lawn chairs sectioned into rows sit vacant by the corner of the wall. I settle into one and Jilly joins beside me. The day is quiet. A breeze emerges from within the wall's shadow as birds chirp and fly overhead. I rest into the chair taking a deep breathe while studying the highest peak of the wall.

We sit in silence. I reflect on my current emotions and start to dissect every segment of my life. I'm unhappy in the city I live in. I'm unhappy in my job. I'm unhappy in my love life at home. I'm almost twenty-four years old, approaching twenty-five next year. Is this what a "quarter-life crisis" consists of? Unhappiness in every aspect of my life? Is this why I feel stuck? I am falling under this classification because I have chosen to live a life I'm not happy with. There is no one to blame but me. If I want to change that, I have to do it myself.

‹ing about?" Jilly asks.

ɔud, I feel my body start to break down. like I am at a standstill in my life and ‡hange that without making the wrong ‡aking a risk means there is a probability of success aɪ... ɔ. But am I ready if failure hits and the road leads to nowhere? I only take roads to destinations. I always follow the GPS. Do I go off course to see what may be out there for me? Or do I stay where I am and try to make my life work at home… I just don't know anymore." I bury my face in my hands.

"You need to get out of Miami. I think that is your first answer. You know you want to. Just pick a place. Come to New York!" she suggests.

"New York is not for me right now. If there is any place I feel more comfortably connected to it's here, in Israel. Does that make me sound insane? Mr. GQ even asked me to come here and swim in his pool in Eilat! I died." I start to laugh through my tears.

"Oh my God, stop."

"I swear," I continue, "My whole life I was programed to think that success was only achieved through how much money I make. And I saved a shit ton of money living at home. But now, I meet Mr. GQ and I have never felt more deeply connected to a person, whom I just met, in my entire life. He makes me feel whole; he makes me feel alive instead of just content. I'm struggling with figuring out what is important at this age in my life right now. Is it focusing on finding love, getting married and having a family? Or is focusing solely on building a career and making a lot of money? I have only focused on a career and money in the past. Now, I have a totally different mindset on what I thought I wanted."

"I know this is a hard decision and you have a lot of factors to consider, but you need to slow down and analyze one thing at a time. We know you have always wanted to move. Maybe this is your wake up call to finally do it. Selfishly, I would love for you to come to New York. Everyone on this trip lives there and you would find a job in a heartbeat! If you know you have this kind of support, what is there to be afraid of?" She asks.

"The risk," I confess, "but I guess that's why I need to take one."

I don't like taking risks. I never have. This is the reason why I live a life of safety. I am preset to think that being content is healthier than living a life of self-fulfillment. I now disagree. I need to take a risk. It is the only way to move out of this state of internal unhappiness. I need to form a plan. The hardest part will be to actually follow through with it. My first plan of action will have to start with my job.

I have a lot of concerns with my position that young professionals at the same point in my career have. All employees at my company are twice my age, which is not the main issue; I love adults. The issue is that my supervisors still view and treat me as the twenty-one year-old, postgraduate who still lives at home. I am not recognized for my worth as a hard working twenty-three year old who wants to grow within the company. Age should not predicate performance, yet ageism still exists as workplace concern. I want to reshape this classification for young professionals who earn their right to grow, without being categorized under another negative generalization of being born a millennial. I was never a victim of giving up, so if I had to start anywhere with change, it would have to begin with my job.

I take one last deep breath, wiping away any stale tears, reminding myself that I will be okay. I know it won't be easy, but I know it will be worth it. Trekking back to the vicinity of the bus, I am one of the last to board. There he stands. Looking cool, calm, and collected as he waits with his back against the side door smiling towards me. His hands rest in his pockets. I wonder if this is why he is a Commander. Giving orders, taking action, all the while making it look natural, as if nothing was a big deal, even if buildings were crashing down behind him.

I walk up to him and he passes me a red string. "Will you tie this on for me, please?"

"Will you always remember I tied it on you?" I ask.

"I will until it breaks. Then, you will have to come back to tie on the next one," he smiles.

I laugh, "You've got yourself a deal."

Since this was our last day in Jerusalem, our tour guide and group leader decide to stray from our itinerary to go to Machane Yehuda Market, a delicious, colorful market that would make Fresh Market only wish they were this fresh. An

Instagram foodie's dream in the Middle East with a mecca of munchies and my favorite, free samples. We launch off the bus and our guide orders, "Be back in one hour at this spot." One hour! One hour is not enough time. Jilly and I head straight for the freshly hand rolled rugelach stand. Watching drips of chocolate cascade down the side of the tray, I want to smear my finger across the edge, but luckily, before I give in to my urge, the owner asks if we would like to try a sample. Besides free, my second favorite word is sample. My smile expands larger than it ever has before. I gladly accept.

As I was about to purchase an entire box, Mr. GQ grabs the wallet from my hand and stuffs it in his back pocket. With fumes coming out of my ears, I turn to him, "Don't you know it is impolite to pause an eager food related purchase from a woman?" I shout. "There is so much more to see. Trust me, you would rather taste the whole market than waste your appetite on a box of this," he argues throwing the box back on the counter. "I'm sorry, I don't think you understand… waste and rugelach are not in the same category. This is heaven. Let me introduce you. Welcome," I smile, showcasing my rugelach. "Let me prove you wrong. I want to show you the market through my eyes. Just you and me," he signals for my hand. Ok, fine. How could I say no to that proposal? I'm pretty sure I was dying in the rugelach heaven I was already in. "Ok, hold on." I run back to Jilly to let her know I'm going on Aladdin's magic carpet ride and may never come back. She smiles, "Have fun kids!"

Arm in arm, we walk through the market tasting different types of olives, halvah, cherries, baklava, and foreign pastries from the Middle East. Even though some foods did look questionable, he fed them to me anyway, and I loved it.

"Just watch. I'll lead."

And I do watch. How he interacts with strangers shaking every vendors hand. How his eyes smile when he takes his first bite. The way he carefully listens when he learns something new. How he speaks to strangers' souls even over the consistency of pita bread. He is special. I admire his excitement in introducing me to new things, while describing the essence of each flavor and aroma. He taught me how to slow down. To savor each bite and appreciate each moment. I feel present. Time does not exist when I am with him.

"Taste it. Chew slowly. Feel the texture. Taste the nuts in there? I know, it's so good," he describes with handful passion.

Rows of spices, fruits, candy, herbs. We are like kids in an adult candy store, buying and tasting, buying and tasting. We explore through our senses and through our pallets. Him and I as one. He picks and places each bite upon my tongue. I never wanted to be that couple, until I met him.

"Can I show you something?" he asks. "You lead, I watch," I tease. "Very good. It requires climbing a few flights of stairs. Are you up for it?" This kid definitely has a thing for stairs and rooftops! "Your relationship with stairs is unlike anything I have ever seen before. Let's do it," I answer.

He grabs my hand and we run through the aisles of the market until we reach an abandoned-looking building. Normally, I would never go inside a place like this, but he told me to trust him, so I do. He runs upwards and I skip steps to catch up, my heart rate skyrocketing with each stride. Definitely buying that well deserved box of rugelach when we get back down from here. We finally reach the top. There is no breeze and I feel the under boob sweat start to drip.

"Ready?" he asks. "Yes," I say, hunched over to catch my breath while trying to put myself back together again. He reaches down for a kiss and opens the door. The initial breeze is everything. Then, I open my eyes, and it is maybe the shittiest rooftop I have ever seen, but what sold him was the view.

The wall is high. He lifts me onto a garbage pail to sit above the barrier. I dangle my legs as he comes up behind me. Pressing his chest against my back, he wraps his arms around me. I lay my head against his shoulder and close my eyes, breathing in the fresh air of the sky and his scent.

The wind frequently blows through my hair, as sounds rise from below. We take a look over the ledge to see a violinist starting to play. I look at him, "Are you kidding me, did you plan this?" I ask. "I swear I didn't," he laughs. "Just enjoy it. It was meant to be." He leans his chin beside mine.

Meant to be. Those words hit me hard. I feel like I am living in a real-life fairytale, wistfully hoping for the happy ending that would probably not end so happily for me. It is going to end. It will end tomorrow. Tomorrow will be his last day with us and then what will I do? After getting to know him, really know him, from the first day I saw him step out of a magazine cover, I had the cake and ate it too. But now there's nothing left. This is the part of the love story they don't prepare you for.

We see our group collect in the distance and notice the time; we only have ten minutes left. "One last dance with me?" he asks. Hiding behind my hands, I feel the blush rising to the surface, "Are you real? I just need to know. Your romantic meter has reached its peak." "My meter doesn't have a peak. It's unlimited," he says. "Infinite," I correct. "Infinite," he repeats.

We dance, our bodies connect and I feel the moment in every detail. His heartbeat echoes as I rest close to his chest. My uncontrolled tears start to fall. This connection, more powerful than any outside force I have witnessed lives deeply within me. Tomorrow, all of this will vanish, as distant as a dream. How could it be that in such a short amount of time, I think I have fallen in love with him?

The violin stops playing and the audience below applaud.

"Are you ready?" he asks, before dipping me and planting an extended, passionate kiss. "10 out of 10. You have officially redeemed yourself." "Yes! My life's mission is complete. You can buy your chocolate now," he says before racing down the steps to our group.

I walk back to Jilly and take a peek inside her shopping bags to see what goodies she is hiding. Mmm candy. I will be picking at that pile later. Waiting for the bus to come, we see a merchant selling individual flowers. Our friend Sam buys a yellow chrysanthemum for his girlfriend and we all admire his sweet gesture. Mr. GQ calls me over to share a smoothie he just purchased. I skip to his side and take the cup noticing he's hiding something behind his back.

"Whatchya got there?" I ask. He places his hand on my face and gives me the flower. "For you, my little *perach*." I stand frozen in disbelief, basking in this garden of joy. "For me, really?" No one ever buys me flowers. He sips his smoothie and leans back on the railing with one foot resting on the fence. "I know. I'm romantic. Get used to it," he walks off.

It doesn't take a lot of work or creativity to impress me. I think guys get the wrong impression when they meet me, expecting me to expect more, but I really expect less. My love tank fills on quality time, not gifts. Anything in addition to that is a treat for me. If I want something, I buy it myself. But one thing you can't buy is time. Mr. GQ has filled my tank with all the right objects. Affection. Care. Comfort. Joy. Surprise. Challenge. Love. I take in the scent and can't control my smile. I hold the flower in one hand, not letting go of his hand in the other.

Tonight will be the last night I will spend with him. Tomorrow will be the last day I will see him. This is a hard pill to swallow. I still can't comprehend how this came about but I am glad I gave him the chance to open a gate to my heart that has been locked open-endedly for some time.

The group gathers in the lobby to discuss our activities for tomorrow. I find an empty chair and he places himself on the floor between my legs. I look down at him and take in his every feature. His chiseled jaw, broad shoulders, big hands, and the addictive scent of his cologne emanating off his skin. The group reflects on this past week and the relationships we have formed. How we began as strangers and ended with solidified strong bonds. Our leaders prepare us for an emotional day tomorrow, giving us the opportunity to share any thoughts, feelings, and intuitions.

At the bar area we buy cups of coffee and walk outside to the patio, posting against the iron railing. "Are we going to be spending an all-nighter out here?" he asks. "I've actually never spent an all-nighter. I value my beauty sleep," I answer. "I've experienced countless all-nighters working on the ship. Sometimes twenty-six hours, sleep for four hours, work again another twenty hours. It's crazy," he explains. "And not one little wrinkle on that face of yours. Your genetics are top notch," I jest. "Yeah," he laughs, "my Israeli-British blood combo." "I'll say… Shall we go for a walk?" I ask. "I actually have a surprise for you. Come with me," kissing my hand before taking it in his, he leads me up the steps. Another surprise. His gifts are endless. Not to mention the calf workout I've gotten with all of this stair climbing. He pauses in front of his room and turns to the left. This is the vacant room we were in yesterday. Now it's locked. He puts a key into the door and it opens. How did he…?

"Surprised?" he asks, revealing a bed covered in white roses, while I secretly have another heart attack inside. My feet are stagnant from where I stand. "What? How did you… I'm so confused. How did you do that?" I ask. "Come in," he says. "Wait. Seriously. How did you do that?" I point to the door. "I went to the front desk and told them my room key didn't work. He asked me what room I was in. I said 505, so he changed my room key to this room," he explains. "Shut the fuck up!" I'm in awe. "So, you're telling me that somehow with your miraculous charm, you went to the front desk and asked him to assign you keys to an empty room that no one is staying in, that you are not paying for?" I ask. "Yes," he says. "How does that even happen?" I ask. "What you said, with my charm," he smiles.

He pulls me inside the room and swiftly lifts me onto the bed. He takes out his phone and starts playing music while I lay down, smelling each layer of petals.

He lies beside me and I immediately get lost in his eyes. He pulls me closer. My face now inches from his as he hovers his body over mine, leaning in for a kiss. I breathe in his scent, feeling the soft texture of his lips and the shape of his muscular form. I peel off his shirt, grazing his back, similar to a Greek sculpture molded by the Gods. His large, high tempered hands explore my body as he makes his way from my lips to my chest. He maneuvers himself underneath me while moving his hands up my thighs. I begin to lift my dress overhead until he stops me.

"We will not do this unless you want to do this," he says. "I want to do this," I express. I want nothing more than to soulfully and physically connect his body with mine.

Resting at my neck, he gathers the bottoms of my dress seam, rolling the fabric around his wrists until I'm pulled down onto his chest. He turns me onto my back as he slides my undergarments down my thighs, getting lost in the sheets. Tenderly, he traces the beat of my pulse with his mouth. His breath panting from my neck to my chest as he lowers below. His fingertips glide up my sides passed my shoulders until my dress falls onto the floor. "That's how you are supposed to undress a woman," he whispers. We make love and I feel like it was the first time, as a woman, I made real love to a man.

I lie next to him, unclothed, with my skin attached to his. The room is dark with the natural glow of night shining in through the window. His face luminous in the light's shadow. His arm pulls me in close to his ribcage as he nestles his chin in my neck. I can feel his breathing as if it is my own. I turn over to look at him and, with one final kiss, I wish him good-night. An overwhelming feeling of love and attachment fill my bones. This night, the best night of my life, will be my last night with him.

Some people believe that the strongest human connection exists in the form of a soul mate. I never thought I would meet my match, until I notice I was lying beside it. I want to keep him. That is the one part I don't know how to do.

I wake up from an uninterrupted sleep cradled in his hold. I always feel most comfortable sleeping alone. This time, the heat of one's body did not bother me. The sweat from his chest did not bother me. His body on mine did not bother me. The fit feels just right. I sneak out of his grip and tiptoe to the bathroom lightly patting the skin around my eyelids. While trying to waken my blood cells, I wipe away the bits of black mascara that had fallen underneath my eyes. Returning to the bed, I look around for my garments and quietly begin to dress. He starts to move slowly beneath the covers and looks up furrowing his brow. "No. You are not leaving yet. Come here," he demands. He grabs hold of my waist and lifts me on top of him. He kisses the sides of my cheeks approaching my lips as I fall beneath him. "I see what you are trying to do here, but I have to pack my things upstairs. Today's our last day I need to grieve," I disclose.

He presses his weight against me, begging me not to leave. I can feel every muscle of his body harden on top of me. Running the tip of his nose against mine and across my cheek he tucks his head into my shoulder. "How could you want to leave this right now?" he pleads. "Why do you look gorgeous when you wake up it's not fair," I respond. He lifts his head and pouts, "Still gorgeous now?" he asks.

I peck his cheek and roll his body off of mine to head for the door. How am I leaving this sexy, naked man, sprawled out on the bed beneath tangled sheets? He rests against his arm spreading his legs apart until his foot leans off the edge. "If looks could kill," I confess to him. He starts to slowly lower the sheets from his body, "Good enough for you to come back to bed?" he asks. "More than enough." I pick up his shirt and toss it on his chest, "See you in an hour," I shut the door.

I sprint back to my room making sure no one catches my morning flee. I find the girls asleep, so I jump on Jilly's bed to shake her awake. She rubs her eyelids open to find me hovering above her. "Hi," I greet. "Hi" she pauses, "You smell like sex." "Ew. Do I really? What does sex smell like?" I sniff. "Sex," she replies. "Oh. I was hoping it would smell like roses or Febreeze calming meadow scent but, guess not," I say, "I'm going in the shower."

"How was it?" she asks. I exhale, "Magical." "Your skin is glowing from all of this 'magic'," she says, smiling. "Oh is it?" I look in the mirror. "Did anyone witness your walk of shame?" she asks. "You mean walk of success?" I correct her, "No. I came, I saw, I conquered." "It definitely looks like you did. Nice bruises," she baits.

"What!" I shout.

The Last Kiss

I walk back to the table with a full plate of watermelon all for myself. There is something about Israeli watermelon that is so fresh, juicy, and defined in its color. It's impossible to refuse, even with a food baby. 'It's just water' I like to tell myself... 1,000 grams of sugar later.

"Are you building a watermelon fortress?" Jilly asks.

"One will be built soon inside my stomach. They just don't grow them like they do here. I can't explain it. I could live in and eat this watermelon for the rest of my life," I express.

"You're going to turn into one at this rate," Dana says.

"My ass and my chest are already a total of four watermelons. Won't be hard for the rest of the team to follow," I convince. "Well, anyway... how was last night? I need details. Have you spoken about what will happen after he leaves?" Jilly asks.

"Negative," I answer.

"Why not?" she asks.

I shrug my shoulders and continue to eat. Of course I want to see where this goes! How could I possibly not?! I fell in, and out, and back into love these past couple of days. I don't think I will ever meet someone like him again. I am more than willing to take a chance on us to see where this will go. I only need to find out if his heart feels the same.

Stuffing the last bite of watermelon in my mouth, I stand to leave and my stare fixates on the entrance as my beautiful mortal walks through the door in full uniform. If you predicted that the piece of watermelon fell out of my mouth as my jaw dropped, you would be correct. He looks like the newest version of a Navy Edition Ken doll, but better looking, with an accent. I always assumed Ken was American with a killer tan, but I *clearly* was mistaken.

To think that only a few days ago, I was afraid to approach him because he seemed too perfect for comfort, but now, I line straight for him, basking in his perfection that I have branded to be mine. He is beautiful. He is strong. He is my man in uniform.

Knowing it would be my last breakfast with him, I take advantage of the time, and wrap my arms around his shoulders, letting him take hold of my waist to shift me onto his lap. I imprint his face in my mind, taking a mental picture of the way his eyes scrunch on both sides when he grins. How he lifts his chin and squints before asking me what I'm thinking. Oh, what I would do to fall asleep and wake up beside him every day. To fulfill this dream, I would have to give up everything. Was everything worth giving up for this feeling?

Watching him lift my apartment-sized luggage into the carriage makes the departure feel very real. I slide into our row, the one from the first day, as he sits beside me and snugs me into the corner. We rest upon the seats facing each other. His forehead touching mine.

"Shit, this is going to be a hard day," I murmur. "I know," he pauses, "can I just say, it's weird for me, too. I didn't expect this to be to the extent of what it became. I cared for you very, very quickly and that's never really happened before. I will miss your face very much," he bids me a long kiss. He rests back into his chair and looks at the ceiling.

"What am I going to do with you?" he asks. "I don't know," I say, nervously picking apart my nail until he firms his hands over mine. "Tell me what you're thinking?" he asks.

"I don't want to say," I hesitate. "Why not? When has that ever stopped you?"

I hesitate, not knowing if I should tell him my thoughts. Would it make a difference either way? "I am so fulfilled and at bliss with you that I don't want to go back to my reality. Your reality is here. So everything stays the same for you. You live here, you work here, your friends, your family, your life, is all here. At home, I felt like I was missing one thing. I didn't know what it was, so I avoided thinking about it. Being with you made me realize you were that thing. God plays tricks on us and this feels like one of them. We are in two different places on two different paths, in two different countries and our hearts exploded." "What happens after an explosion?" he asks. "Basically, everybody dies," I respond. He laughs. "Nobody is going to die here," he stares into both of my eyes. "A theoretical death," I correct him.

"You find what matters most to you and that becomes your new beginning. Life will go back to normal, eventually, but in the process we learn what is worth living for," he admits, "Look we're here," he points out the window.

The bus stops at the top of the hill in front of the Yad Vashem Memorial. Yad Vashem is one of the most renowned Holocaust museums in the world, and although I've been here a few times, this visit is different. All I can think about is leaving him. I hold onto him as we explore, just him and I, behind the rest of the group.

Walking through the halls, I feel lonely in my thoughts and selfish for not immersing myself in this vast history. All I can think about is our own history, and how much had changed over such a short span of time. Yesterday, I was just a young girl fascinated by a young man. Today, I am a woman in love with that man. I try to hold myself back from clinging to his side. I know that he feels the same. He glances behind to reach for my hand, where I normally stood. I turn to glimpse if he is following behind, which he regularly was. I find myself shadowing his every movement, as I could not bear being physically apart.

Leaving the museum, we ride through a nearby neighborhood to stop for lunch. While searching for places to eat, he asks to take me out to lunch, just the two of us. "Is the Commander asking me out on a proper date?" I tease. "Yes. I am asking you out on a date. Are you going to reject my offer?" "Well that depends, where do you want to take me?" I excite. "You said your favorite food is sushi," he points to the restaurant behind us, "would you like to go?" he asks. "I would be delighted to share a sushi roll with you," I beam.

We walk into the restaurant and are prepared a booth. I slide in first and he follows alongside me. The urge to stay beside him, touching him, feeling his skin next to mine becomes stronger and stronger. I am not going to handle this goodbye well.

"Do you want to know something interesting?" he asks. "Always," I take a sip of my water. "My grandparents live in the building next door," he discloses. I stop drinking and look up at him, "No way! Do they really?" "Yes. I haven't seen them in a very long time. Will you come meet them with me?" he asks while continuing to indulge in his roll. I sit still. "Really?" Is he serious? "Like, are you sure?" "Yes, I'm sure. You are special to me and I want you to meet them," he traces my cheek.

Oh God. Here is a theoretical death in the making. Meeting the fam before leaving in five hours? I can't handle this. Are these the British grandparents or Israeli grandparents? Do they speak English or Hebrew? Fuck the future heartbreak. "Of course, I would be honored to meet them," I decide. "Great. That means a lot to me," he says.

This just became very real. I am meeting his grandparents in a tank top and shorts from Target, wearing Nikes and a Prada. I wish I were more dressed up to fit the part. I cannot believe this is about to happen. I am full and nervous but more so full.

Upon fishing our lunch, we exit the restaurant and turn the corner. The building is literally connected next door. Walking beneath floral pots we enter through the glass doors and sign in at the front desk. Beyond the lobby stands a wooden stained pergola wrapped in vines with gardens on each side. Bougainvillea peek through the Jerusalem stone columns. This is a *very* upscale old age home. I could totally be an elder here. He realigns his shirt and belt before the elevator opens. We ride up to the ninth floor and he continues to fix himself in the mirrored panels. Why is he so on edge? This is unfamiliar.

The elevator opens and we walk to the last door at the end of the hall. He stops.

"Before we go in, I just want to thank you for coming with me. This is a little hard for me because I haven't seen them in over a year and my grandmother may not recognize who I am. She has Alzheimer's disease. I just want you to know in case things get confusing," he confesses.

"Ok," I nod, taken aback by his vulnerability.

I grab his hand. He sighs and looks over at me before knocking on the door. An older, white haired man with large spectacles greets us in a red sweater vest. "Look who it is!" he throws his hands up in surprise and excitement. An English accent. Phew. He is one of the Brits. Excellent. We should get along very well.

His grandfather gives both of us a hug before we walk through the door. His grandmother sits on the couch and initially thought he was his older brother. He did not correct her while embracing her petite frame and wearing a wistful smile. When he introduces me to her, I give her a hug. She is absolutely delightful. She walks me through each family photo that covers the walls. Baby photos, graduation photos, photographs of grandsons being sworn into the army. I cannot believe I am here. I cannot believe I am with his grandparents. They admit they can't believe it either. This is their first time seeing him wearing full uniform in person.

We take a seat in their living room and his grandfather asks how Mr. GQ's parents are doing. I can't help but look around at every trinket that fills the apartment. "What are your plans after your naval service?" he asks. "I am not sure yet," he answers. "Why don't you travel or live in England for a while? When was the last time you visited?" his grandfather asks. "A very long time ago. And no, I will stay in Israel. Israel is my home," he answers. "But you can always come back here. You have a world to see and to live," his grandfather continues. "Israel is my home. I don't need to leave," he finalizes. His grandfather turns to me, "And how about you? How did my grandson meet a nice American girl like you?"

We catch each other's stare and smile. "He asked if a seat was taken, which it was, and I made room for him. More than once." "Romantic he is. He must have learned that from me," he says. Mr. GQ laughs and agrees. "What do you do in the states? Where do you see yourself next?" his grandfather asks. "I plan conferences for doctors. As for the future, this is the first time I really don't know," I answer honestly. "Would you ever think of moving away, maybe to Israel?" he asks. Before I can answer, Mr. GQ tilts his head in anticipation, shifting his body to face me, while waiting for my response.

"If that is what I wanted to do in that moment in time, I would consider it. But it would have to be for a reason well worth giving up everything for," I reply.

He smiles approvingly and shifts back to his original demeanor. Realizing the time, Mr. GQ announces we must head out. He gives his grandparents long farewells. Just before we leave, his grandmother calls his name and wishes for him to be safe. He nods giving thanks, and I notice his eyes swell. She remembered his name.

Four hours. Four hours left until we have to say good-bye. I never had a problem with saying goodbye, but today feels like a funeral. We walk in silence entering Mount Herzl, Israel's national cemetery, reading the names of fallen soldiers engraved on the walls and tombstones. Mr. GQ asks if he can read me something. I happily agree. He takes out a piece of paper from his pocket. It is an article about the INS Dakar memorial, a site he will be speaking to our group about. This memorial displayed in Mount Herzl, honors sixty-nine naval soldiers who lost their lives on the Dakar submarine. After the submarine's first voyage, it disappeared without a trace. The Israeli army initiated an extensive rescue operation with their ships and airplanes to find Dakar and its crew. It was not found until thirty years later near Crete, Greece. Those sixty-nine names are engraved inside of the submarine-shaped memorial.

He shares that this is not only important to him because of his position in service, but is also important because his friend's brother had passed away while serving in the navy. He explains how this brother was like his own, and he wants to honor him the best that he can.

A few sentences into reciting his prepared words, he stops. Tears begin to fall from his face. I gently wipe each tear away not wanting others to see. Folding the papers and placing them back in his pocket, he decides that the words will come to him when it is time.

We walk past the multiple benches that line the stone pathway. He taps his hand on my waist and signals to sit beside him. I sit silently, overcome with emotion from being in a burial site filled with young soldiers, like him. If I'm already struggling with sensitizing my emotions, I can't begin to imagine what he may be feeling.

He leans on my shoulder and I clench his hands in mine. I am grateful to be able to be his support.

Our group turns in the distance and disappears. He wipes his face and leads the way to the Dakar memorial. I hand him tissues from my backpack but he shoos them away. "As I teach my soldiers, real men cry and should not be ashamed of it." A beautiful truth. If only he could teach that to all the men in the world.

Walking in one by one, we fill the circular shape of the submarine. Everyone is silent and waits for Mr. GQ to begin his delivery. Unfolding his naval cap, he places it on his head and retrieves the paper from his pocket.

His voice is low and soft while he stutters through his emotive speech. It pains me to watch him suffer through his emotions while trying to tell his story. I can't imagine the combat of thoughts in his head. This could have been him. This could have been any one of his soldiers. To watch him grieve in front of our group, without being able to comfort him, left me feeling helpless.

He turns away from us gliding his hand across the inscribed names on the wall. The group starts to disperse towards the exit but I hold back to wait for him. I try to keep my distance. I can tell he needs more time here and I want him to have it. As he walks in my direction, I have the urge to unleash my tears, but I fight back to be strong for him. Holding me tight to his chest, he doesn't have to say anything for me to know, I'm exactly where he needs me to be.

Our group leader motions for us to continue and we begin to leave the tunnel. We reach the spot where the sun reflects off the ceiling. He looks back one last time and asks to be alone. I nod and walk ahead when I turn and see him fall to the floor. He clutches his knees to his chest. I struggle under the weight of his pain, wishing I could help him but knowing that I can't.

I wait beyond the walls gazing at the other memorials in this division. Eighteen, nineteen, twenty-one, twenty-three, twenty-six years old. Soldiers my age gone in war. As Americans who are not required from birth to enroll in the army, we can neither relate nor imagine the experience of having to provide protection for your country at such a young age. Parents having to prepare their children. Brothers and sisters having to guide their siblings. It's like being thrown into the deep end when you don't know how to swim and knowing that you have only two options: to sink or to swim. There is no other choice but to try to survive.

The footsteps behind me feel closer. He rests his arm on my shoulder and surprises me with a kiss. "Let's go," he murmurs. We walk silently following the stone trail until we meet the rest of the group. Our guide points to one gravestone and then another, telling the stories of each life that was lived and will forever be remembered. I rest beneath the shaded wall to keep an eye on Mr. GQ and an ear on them.

Running his fingers across every stone, he wanders through each aisle reading every passage. He picks up a handful of rocks at the end of the row placing one on each passing edge. He comes to a stop and squats down, pulling a chest out from the header of a memorial. I wonder if he will open it.

Twisting the bolt, he unlocks the top exposing what lies underneath. Piles of pictures and notes. He stares at each photo and reads the opposite side. He must have closely filtered through fifty pieces, with a continuous stream of tears down his cheeks.

I want to console him but I remain in the shade. Watching him fall apart behind these stones shatters my heart into a million pieces. I've never known a heart break like this before. I feel deeply that this could be him. Such young soldiers. All our age. This could be any one of us in their place. I cannot fathom imagining anything ever happening to him. If it ever did, it would be one of the greatest losses my heart has ever witnessed. This is why it feels like a funeral. I can't imagine losing him.

I realize deeply in this moment that I love him. In the shortest amount of time, with the good and the bad, I loved all of him. With this feeling, I knew if anyone had to make a sacrifice for another, I would willingly sacrifice my life back home to be with him. I think back to how I was always afraid to be married. Always thinking that I would settle for love, never actually fall into it. But then I met him. Allowing to give my whole self to him was a hard choice at the beginning. Now that we are at the end, I cannot possibly imagine any other way I would have wanted it. I was not ready to leave him. I could not leave him. I could not even picture my life without him.

One by one we exit out of the memorial. I follow behind him. Without looking back, he wraps my arms around his waist holding me in. Knowing I was minutes away from saying goodbye, uncontrollable tears drown out my breathing. My heart rate peaks and my chest pounds massively, terrified of leaving him. Holding him tightly, I never want to let go.

At the beginning of this journey, I had no expectations. I had nothing to lose. Now, being intensely involved with him, I feel that I have everything to lose. I still can't comprehend how this manifested, but he has become everything to me. Like in a dream, an angel dropped before me and I danced with him until he sailed out of my reach. Now I am left broken, broken-hearted, where each crack is etched permanently into stone.

All I can focus on is breathing while I gaze down at our footsteps. Meeting his eyes is too painful. My chest feels tight with pain. Before the bus pulls forward, we sit in a circle for our last group exercise: saying goodbye to the soldiers. Strangers in this circle. That's all we once were. Traveling as a group from New York. Adopting soldiers into our unit once we touched land. We were all just strangers. Strangers who became family so quickly, in just a matter of days. Now, having to say our goodbyes, by life's nature, we become strangers again. For me, this exercise feels like a lesson on how to say goodbye to the one you love. A lesson I just can't complete. I sit beside him as he cradles my hands in his. Still unable to bring my gaze up from the floor, I forbid an eruption of tears from being his last mental picture of me.

Without knowing this feeling ever existed, I finally start to understand it. You can't think. You can't breathe. You physically can't be. With love you are full, without it you are empty. I have become a believer of love and heartbreak in the shortest amount of time, but I was not given the tools on how to mend it.

I watch each of my friends hug the soldiers' goodbye, while singing songs swaying in a growing circle. I need to find the right words for a proper farewell before we say our final goodbye. Even if it takes an hour, I am not leaving this pavement. He stands before me with a firm grip on my shoulders and I still can't bring myself to meet his eyes. This is the last time I will feel his touch. The last time I will hear him breathe. The last time I will mirror his stare. My fierce cry halts the words that are developing from my mouth. I take in a shattered deep breath and release.

"Bear with me," I joke in advance through my tears. "I can't express how thankful I am that our worlds came together so unexpectedly. I have never been more myself with another person. You have taught me something new that I will hold on to forever. You taught me how to love and to know what it feels like to be loved. I can only wish in my lifetime that I will meet someone as amazing as you. You fully accepted me for me and showed me why life is worth living. Whatever happens between us, I will never forget you and I will miss your smile every day. You changed my life and I am so thankful that you fought to be in it. I came on this trip as one person and I am leaving as another. No one will ever be able to fill the space you have created in my heart and I am so appreciative to have known who you really are," I confess. I find the courage to meet his eyes with his tears reflecting mine.

He presses his thumbs against my cheeks and wipes away the excess. Planting a kiss on my lips, he takes hold of my hands.

"My love, you are truly as special as I first thought. I was not supposed to come here and now I know why I was. To meet you. Thank you for giving me your heart and a chance to show you who I am. Thank you for letting me in, as hard as you tried to keep me out. I have never met anyone like you before and you are truly your own person. Keep spreading that smile of yours across the world so everyone can see how amazing you are. I know our lives are demanding and we live in different places, but there is something about this that I cannot explain that I don't want to just give up on. I don't want you to find another me, but whoever that person will be, he will be the luckiest man in the world. And if he messes it up I will kill him myself. Just send me his address," he tales.

"Very funny. I know a few people if you want a head start," I joke.

I can't believe this is goodbye. I won't accept this as good-bye. How could two people leave each other's lives just because of different time zones? How can we make this work? I want to make this work.

He lifts up my chin, "We don't have to stop talking, you know. We can continue and if there is a way to see each other again, we will. If you meet someone else, you let me know. If I meet someone else, I will let you know. We can try this so that at least we can say we tried," he says.

"Really?" I light up. "Yes," he confirms.

I wrap my arms around his shoulders and mount him with a kiss, "Thank you." "For what?" he asks.

"For giving me one last minute of sanity before you walk away and I crumble into a thousand pieces," I say.

"Stay strong for me and I will stay strong for you. I am one text away." Our lips touch for the last time and he the distance.

Even with this inch of hope, my tears carry me to sleep as we arrive in Tel Aviv. We settle in at the hotel and I sink beneath the covers. Tonight is our last night out, but I can't even think about partying or socializing. I want to stay in bed alone to grieve the seven stages of possibly never seeing him again. Jilly comes into the room with a gifted bottle of wine and pours both of us a glass. "Get your ass out of bed. This is not the girl I know and raised. We're going out," she says.

I tap the puffiness around my eyes with my fingertips, "I am not going out." She rips the covers off my body. "Drink this right now. Wine cures whine," she demands.

She forces the glass in my hand and I take a sip. Not bad for cheap wine. I sit up and wipe my face, consuming half of the glass's contents. She plays some music and pulls me out of bed. Pushing me towards the shower, she passes me a refilled glass before shutting the door. Leaning my palms against the cold countertop stills me. I can't even meet my face to look in the mirror, but I know that sitting here in sorrow will only feed the heartache. I can't believe this happened to ME. I sip the last drop hoping for good juju to kick in. I turn the knob to test the waters waiting for the steam to fill up the glass so I can't see my reflection. I can cry one last time in there without anyone knowing. Hopefully my emotions will fall with the water into the drain.

I step into the shower and feel the hot rhythm of water massage my back. The steaming pellets touch my skin and I feel nothing. My eyes are closed with empty thoughts and I'm drained of all my energy. Just thinking his name sets me off into another sobbing frenzy. The only thing I can feel is bad for myself. Bad that I want to shake myself out of this funk and I don't know how to reverse it. Bad because I know the only person who can help me is myself and I haven't read the manual on that yet.

I step onto the chilled tile underneath me. I wrap myself in a towel looking in the mirror at my blotchy, red eyes, swelling the surface of my cheeks. I pour cool water on my face until the heat dissipates from my skin. Breathing normally feels difficult, but I take my glass and walk back into the room to ask for another.

Jilly curls her hair to the beat of the music when she smiles back at me in the reflection of the mirror. "Refill?" she asks with a wink. I concede. Thank God my best friend is here with me. I feel regretful that we came on this trip to simply spend time together. Then, I flipped our itinerary upside down because of my Naval Avatar. But she wasn't upset with me. She was happy and upset for me. If there is one thing I am incredibly grateful for, it is experiencing this journey with her.

I sit on the floor to blow my hair and attempt to put on some makeup. Trying to stop the tears from falling through my painted lashes is a challenge. Makeup isn't helping the cause, but I need to fix this facial disaster. After getting ready as best as I can, we go to the dinner hall. Despite the delicious looking spread, I can't get myself to eat anything. You know it's a serious matter when I voluntarily choose not to eat.

Our newly turned party bus drives to an outside bar, continuing our escalating alcoholism for the night. I sit across the row from where we used to sit, allowing the melancholy to flood in as it hurts more to hold back, than not acknowledge it at all. One of the girls sits next to me and asks how I am doing. By the look of my expression, I don't feel the need to answer. "Look at this as a beautiful experience," she says, "would you rather not have met him at all? Or have never known what it was like to experience a love like you just did? Some girls don't experience that shit in their lifetime. Consider yourself lucky for feeling feels," she says, trying to lift my spirits. "The unknown of never seeing him again is hard but think about how blessed you were to both meet each other. Don't let this ruin your night. Think of the beauty in it all, not the heartbreak," she pleads.

I nod my head in agreement and thank her for her kind words. I know this emotional behavior is not me. This is not what he wants for me.

It's so much easier to sit in a corner feeling sorry for yourself while wanting to deflect attention. Did I want to sit in a corner alone right now? Of course I did. If we don't allow ourselves to feel our emotions, we will never truly feel and get over what is bothering us. Feel the emotions. Release them. Move on from them. This has to be my motto. No one will make it better but myself. This was another new experiment I had to try on my own.

Jilly takes the drink ticket from my hand and brings back two cold brews from the bar. There is something about cheap tasting beer that brings me cheerful nostalgia from college. Our group pushes large high tops together and I can feel the energy changing. The boys pass the hookah around in a circle while I sip on my cheap beer. I feel the breeze from the ocean and I realize, I am okay. I accept that it's okay to be upset but it's also okay to feel pleasure in moments of heartache.

The guys climb on top of the table and start to move their hips. The girls join shortly after and everyone starts dancing together. It was like Opa coming to life, Israeli style. While the music plays, I hear screams from the bar and look over to see what's going on. My eyes go wide. I must be delusional. But I'm not sure.

He turns around. It's him.

Impossible. I must be unconscious. He walks to the bar and greets our friends, accepting shots until he meets my eye. I sit frozen in my chair facing in his direction. I cannot move a limb. I was mourning the loss of him so deeply that I am now too numb to feel anything other than shock. I turn away from him and finish the rest of my drink to shake off this hallucination. The girls try to push me to walk over to him but I wave them off. They can't possibly understand what I'm feeling. I can't even understand it. Thoughts rush through my head. If I had known he was coming tonight, I wouldn't have had to suffer, knowing I had one more chance to say goodbye, outside of a cemetery. I sit debating which option I would have rather had. To have not seen him again after our goodbye, or to say goodbye one last time after having sat Shiva for six hours.

He makes his way over and cradles my cheeks in his hands, "Hi baby," he says, pressing his lips upon mine, "Surprised?"

I stare blankly. I cannot believe he is standing here. I am actually speechless for the first time. "Dance with me?" he asks, as if nothing has happened. Once he takes my hand, I feel a wave of relief, "What are you doing here?" I ask him.

"I missed you," he winks. "You should have told me you were coming!" I slap his arm, "Do you know what I have been going through since you left?" I shout.

"I'm sorry, I see. I thought it would be a good idea! I'm a romantic remember?" He twirls me around and pulls me in. "I was trying to get over you and now you're here and I have to go through it all again and I am so confused…" I keep blabbering. "Shh, it's okay," he kisses me, "just be with me."

I remember what my friend had told me on the bus. Be present. Let it be. Embrace the experience. He came to surprise me. He came here to be with me. I need to be here with him. Our bodies touch as we dance through the courtyard and drink away into the night.

"Come," he says, "Let's go somewhere alone." I follow him out of the bushes and we walk in the direction of the ocean. The pier stretches for miles, bonding lights glowing at each end. We lean over the railing above the pillars and listen to the waves crash beyond the rocks. I rest my head on his shoulder and look above at the stars.

"Want to jump over and sit?" he points to the oversized rocks. "It's okay. I'm wearing a dress. It's too risky," I say. "I'll carry you. Take my hand." He jumps over the double railing first. I place one foot on the bottom, climbing myself over the top, for him to catch me when I land. I mimic his trail step by step until we reach the largest rock on the bottom of the shore.

The waves flush over the rocks and descend with the tide. My bottom feels cold and grainy on the platform but I am happy to be back in his arms. I sit beside him near dangerous waters splashing against my toes but I feel safe. He runs his hand down the side of my face and I place my hand over his. I shut my eyes wanting to remember this feeling. Surely it will wash away soon with these waves, but at least I have this last memory to hold onto. He extends his arm over to my side and lays me down, shifting my body beneath him. He gifts me one last, long embrace while I soak in his intimacy.

I invite him to spend the night but he doesn't want to push the rules any further. Once the soldiers leave our group they are not permitted to return, but he did. He had to be back at his base tomorrow evening, so I still have one more chance to see him. I reach into his pocket to take out his phone. I open his calendar and add an event:

Time: *10:00 AM*

Location: *Beach with My Love*

"I will see you tomorrow and I won't take no for an answer."

"Ok, Miss Commander. I can see someone is trying to take my position. You can have it," he kisses me deeply into the night. Hours pass and I take in his every breath. His touch. His warmth. His love. I look forward to this in the morning, feeling present with him, one last time.

The sun rises and I sneak away from the group to meet him next to the pink lifeguard house. Leaning against the post in his Ray-Bans and beaming smile makes me melt. I run into his arms as he lifts me to his chest gripping my thighs. This ease of being together is so natural. Being tangled in each other's arms is what I treasure most. Submerged in the water, I study his eyes and never want to forget his stare. I embrace his soft skin upon me and I can't help but think what comes next.

"I can't just let you go and pretend like this never happened," I say.

"It's still happening. We will just have to figure it out," he says.

"But is this really what you want? It's what I want, clearly, but is this what you want?" I ask.

"You are what I want," he nudges my nose, "come back to visit me. Make the time and I will make the time."

Making the time. I ran out of all my PTO days at my job, but I will find a way to make this work. I was going to make this work. We run out of the water and compare our schedules on our phones. Two open weekends. One weekend is my birthday. We can do this. We make the date. I am coming back.

A plan is made and I am willing to put everything on hold to follow it. Knowing that we are taking this chance to test our future is worth the effort and the wait, to see what this love could become. Saying goodbye feels better this time. Not easier, just better. The cracks in my heart are mending as I get his last wind of comfort. I don't cry, but my heart aches, from what feels like my heart walking away.

Prior to boarding the plane I thought, what if I didn't? My world back home felt as if it didn't exist. What only existed was this, here and now. I didn't want to wait to return. I wanted to stay. Sitting at the gate the agent calls the last boarding group. Jilly turns to me and grabs my hand, "It's time. We have to go." I nod. I gather my bags and before walking onto the gateway, I turn back one last time. I will return, I promise myself. I'll make sure of it.

Back in my Miami reality, not one moment passes where I don't think of him. Not one day passes where we don't speak. We can feel each other's presence distances apart. Sleeping in my bed felt lonely and unfamiliar. I craved his touch. His energetic void surrounded me, and my heart held onto his absence. I return to my job a changed person, high on love, but low on life. My ambition at work was to always aim for the highest goal I could achieve. I always knew what I wanted for myself, but now, I wanted something entirely different. I was so blinded by my abundant happiness abroad, that I pushed aside my professional aspirations. The only thing I once cared about has now completely changed its course. My mission was to achieve the highest level of success at work and excel in my position to a level beyond reach. That desire was now thrown out the window. The version of myself pre-Israel would have not agreed to this new mental destination I was traveling toward. The post-Israel version of myself is willing to give it all up to explore more of life's meaning I was introduced to.

At home, work was my life. In Israel, life was my life. The two worlds could not be more separated in my mind. I was leaning more towards the goal of returning to Israel full-time. There, I am the best version of myself. At my job, I am the lesser version of myself. Since I used all of my vacation days on the trip, I fabricate a story to my boss that my cousin was to be wed in Israel and I needed to return. Through pulling teeth, I exchanged the days for unpaid time and it became official. I am returning. Not only will it be a celebration of reuniting with Mr. GQ, it will also be the festivity of my twenty-fourth birthday.

Twenty hours and $2,000 later, I travel back to my heart's home. That is the price and time I was happily willing to invest for love, even if it was just for four days. This time, there are no distractions - just him distracting me.

Mr. GQ reserved a room at the Carmel Forest Spa Resort atop Mount Carmel. It is magical. It is romantic. It is perfect, like no time has passed. Each day we go to sleep and wake up beside one another. We lie by the pool and watch every sunrise and sunset, blending with the natural rhythm of the world. We lie on the daybeds, in the grass, resting in the hammocks while he reads the paper. Nestled in his arms I wish I could live every day like this. I imagine what we could be five years from now. I cherish every passing second, hold onto every minute and hour because this could be my last minute, and hour, in his arms.

We explore each nature trail surrounding the Mount, to sit upon the edge watching the sun descend. Picking flowers from the vines, he weaves stems into my hair. Pulling herbs from the garden, indulging in each scent. He loves his nature and he loves his home. How could I ever ask him to leave it? I won't. The flowers, the leaves, the air and the way the sun set didn't matter back in Miami. It matters here. And it matters to him. Watching him in his element I knew that, unlike him, I could soulfully thrive in both places. I was one person at home and one person in Israel. Living at home, I was a young entrepreneur working two jobs, traveling the country for work. Saving money so that I can invest in the market for a brighter future ahead. And brighter things.

When I began my job at twenty-one years old, it came with a lot of traveling. In and out of different cities all over the US for approximately nine months. My twenty-five-year-old goal remained the same, choose my favorite city I've traveled to and move there for one year. Never did I expand outside of the US to a different country, until now. My twenty-one-year-old mindset was that I would move for myself. This mindset now would be to move for him. If I was going to relocate to Israel and real life did kick in, there is the possibility that we may or may not work out. But the fact that I'm considering going in the first place, far out of my comfort zone, is worth the life lesson to me.

In Israel, I didn't need nice things or the fluff that fills an emotional void in Miami. Here, I treasure every sunset. I savor the music on the street, the breeze against my skin, and the energy that surrounds me. Here, everything is about family and celebrating life together. I want to celebrate life. I am willing to give up my entire life I created to be with this man. I never thought I would move for another, but my world feels nonexistent without him. He feels more important to me than I am to myself. My priorities completely shifted from being a young, head figure in my employment to being whole by just being with him. I didn't see this life working in my hometown. I only saw this life in Israel.

But, what happens when we make plans? We have heard before, God laughs. Because life always finds a way to shake up our steady foundation. Or maybe it is the tremor to bring us back onto our destined paths. We think we are the drivers of our own decisions until we are blinded that we have strayed off track. But God proves that we are merely in the passenger seat, when our plans unexpectedly change course.

My meeting went over time at work, and I missed three of his calls in one hour. The one-hour we set to talk every day, and I periodically am forced to miss it. Work-life balance is always difficult, but I didn't measure how difficult it would be when adding in a relationship with a seven-hour time difference. That day, he decided to end things and it destroyed every living cell in my body.

My heart severed into two and I cried every night beneath my covers. Did I know the end was coming? *-ish.* I knew an ending was possible, but I was too comfortable with our arrangement that my lenses were fogged. Our long distance and unknown future was more difficult for him than it was for me. Even though I mentally prepared for this day to come, my heart could never have prepared for the disruption when it hit.

We talked about a future, a family, and a life in Israel, but never in America. I knew I would be giving up everything and he would be giving up absolutely nothing, but I believed in our love so strongly I trusted that the sacrifice was worth it. I had my entire life already built here. He didn't there. The fact that he didn't know his next step after the army or whether or not to reenlist was the amount of uncertainty for him to break the chord. He couldn't see past the unknown and the time in between. I held space for him in my life but he didn't create a larger space for me to be in his. At least that is what I choose to be true.

I continue to think, *what if* things were different. *What if* I moved sooner? *What if* he was my "one who got away?" I will never stop wondering what could have been, but I need to believe that this happened for a reason. Some say I should feel lucky that I had that "one" in my lifetime. Some don't get to experience this type of love at all. He set a new standard in my heart for the level of love a woman deserves. I never thought I would fall this deep, or that one man had the ability to occupy this newly opened space in my heart, but he forever has, and I don't regret one decision I made.

With or without him, I learned more about myself in those few days to months than I ever had before. I learned how to open my heart and my mind, by sharing my soul with another. I learned the true feeling of real love and painful heartbreak. I recognized the bravery of women choosing to sacrifice their lives to be with a man. Women should be commended for taking that leap, not judged, as I was once guilty of doing before. I learned that life is not about your career, and life is not about making money. Life is about living with all things in love, which is something I had a hard time believing before. All the money and success in the world will never be able to fill the void of love and heartbreak. The only way I knew how to bury this pain, was to turn it into revival in the only way I knew how. I submerged my life instead of in love, fully back into my career.

The universe decides what is and what isn't meant to be. I needed to veer myself back onto the path I walked off of for love. In my mind there was no other choice. Throughout and after college, I've always had tunnel vision. Tunnel vision towards having a great career. I thought once I had earned that success, everything else in love would follow. That obviously never happened. I never created the heart-space. My train only followed the career path I predicted before and now after this love.

Prior to going on Birthright, there was one thing I wanted more than anything in my job. That was to be a manager. I did everything I thought I could to get there but one thing held me back, something I could not change. My age. After losing him, being consumed with nothing more to lose than what I felt I already had, I used that energy to fuel the power within me to never take no for an answer. If I couldn't fight for him, I would fight for the one thing I had more control over, my job.

Resignation

Tunnel Vision

"**A**nd though she be but little, she is fierce." – William Shakespeare.

This is how I always wanted to be defined. Being little was inevitable. Being fierce was instinctive.

For most people, working hard is a choice. For me, it was inherited by genetic nature. Like my parents, I put an equal amount of effort as I do pride into my work. That is one thing no one could ever take away from me.

I began my career as an assistant events coordinator, not an event coordinator's assistant; let's get that straight early on.

On my first day of work, I opened the server and stared at the overwhelming amount of folders, making sure not to transport a file into the wrong one. I was plagued with the common thought, "Can I really *do* this?" But the job became less intimidating once I adopted the mindset: pretend your work is like homework. I was good at homework. I used to sell my assignments for $1.00/page when I was eight years old. Sure, I didn't like the fact that I would spend hours perfecting my work when everyone else was too lazy to finish their own. To this day, I despise lazy people. But if lazy people were willing to pay (in money or sweet treats), I would mind them.

What no one tells you once you secure a job is that there are no agendas, books or cliff notes for how to succeed. You are given your new 10x10 voluntary prison cell, with a, cross your fingers, Mac laptop, and minimal logistic training to then figure everything out on your own.

Through company reorganization, employees quitting, and dumping truckloads of their unwanted work onto me, three people's jobs fell down the ladder into my lap to a state of overwhelming. This happens to every low totem pole new hire in a workplace, but unlike most people, I viewed this as an opportunity, albeit a challenging one, rather than a punishment.

Near the end of my first year, having successfully handled the work, I asked for more responsibilities with contracts, proposals, and event orders. I was awarded the opportunity to manage a few in-house events that I managed successfully, but it was not enough to fulfill my developmental void. After my My Boss viewed my success first hand, I figured asking to be a project manager for larger symposiums would not be an issue. I lived and still live by one mantra: *always ask, the worst they can say is no.* This applies to not only business inquiries, but if you want extra guac for no charge on your taco salad, or a 10% discount off of pre-worn shoes on display, it doesn't hurt to ask. Shopping purchases are still considered a form of business, right? I like to think so.

After proving myself an efficient employee under my department's supervision, I asked My Boss for one thing. Not a raise. Not an office. Not an assistant. I simply asked for more work. More responsibility in exchange for more education. I reached the point of boredom in my position where I knew I could handle more and I wanted to grow. Some workers are happy doing the minimum or their exact title's description, nothing more. That was not how I was bred.

In asking, I figured why wouldn't they want to delegate additional responsibility to a young, eager employee? Wouldn't they rather mold me to advance higher in the company than stay stagnant in the same novice position for ten years? Rhetorical question? I think not. Because stunting my professional growth was my fate, besides already being physically affected at birth.

I asked not once, not twice, not thrice, but *four* times over the span of months to be a project manager by the time I had my second year review, which came directly after my post-Israel honeymoon phase. Walking into her office, I thought to myself if she says no one last time, I'm planning to leave in a year anyway. But if she says yes, I would finally succeed at being persistent about getting what I wanted.

Expect a no, but never accept a no. I continued to receive consecutive no's, but that still didn't keep me from asking. Each time I asked, I was denied. I was denied not for the reason that I was unqualified, because I prove my worth every day. Not because I wasn't a hard worker, I work harder than half of the veterans in here. It was simply because of my age.

The first two times I was denied managerial capabilities I decided I was going to leave the company. I came to terms that wanting to grow was looked down upon. That working hard and taking pride in that work was still not enough to advance. I decided to search for jobs and update my resume to include the current responsibilities in my position. Once I started to write out my duties, as important as they were to the company I worked for, it would not deem as important to another company looking for hire. Therefore I decided I needed to keep trying to be a manager, as I could not leave this company without that experience.

The reason I was introduced to this company was because of Mr. EVP. After graduating college, I had a job lined up through a family friend that, like some things in life that are too good to be true, fell through. For the first time in my life, trusting another person and not having a back up plan left me royally screwed.

After spending two hours parked behind my house, crying a hurricane, I asked God, "Why? Why did this happen to me?" And then I finally realized what I never believed before, that everything does happen for a reason.

I applied to jobs during the day and enrolled in camp Equinox, morning and night, to create a routine for myself so that I wouldn't go insane. This routine unexpectedly landed me my first job.

I was hurrying to the gym for my 5:30 PM Abs Class, when I rushed past my family friend dripping a pool of sweat on the Stairmaster. I had five minutes to spare before entering the class when he asked me when I was going to start my new job.

I explained to him as fast and diligently as possible how I had been trying to find work and couldn't, but was eager to start working. His workout buddy beside him asked what I studied and wanted to do, so I told him and waved off to work on something I could control, my abs.

I am known to be an extremely fast talker because I have a lot to say 99% of the time. Love it or hate it its true, but don't let anyone tell you to slow down (like my future Boss told me) because that is what landed me the job. That night, he called to ask for my resume and the next week I went in for an interview.

I almost didn't take the event coordinator position because I was so disinterested in the medical field. But, based on the empty inbox of responses from my applications, my family friend asked me, "Is anyone else knocking on your door?... Then take the freaking job." So what did I do? I listened to his advice, took the job, and do not regret the decision I made.

My college professor once told my class, "It's not about who you know, it's about who knows you." True and false. In the Jewish community, when we play geography, it's all about who YOU know, *or who knows the people that you know, then that leads you to connect to them.* If it was all about who knows me, I would have been referred multiple, future, potential husbands by now. But that is another discussion for another time. There are opportunities everywhere even when you least expect them. You just have to be there to find them.

Ask and you shall receive is only good advice if you deserve ice cream after getting an A+ on a test in fourth grade. In the real world, when you continue to ask but the door is closed in your face, don't bother continuing to knock. Find a new entrance or push the goddamn door down. And this is what I did. I tapped into my two prominent resources in the company, Mr. EVP and my closest colleague and companion at work, My BFF.

Mr. EVP and I didn't really know each other before I was hired. After getting to know him, I would totally vote for him for President of the United States if he ran. He's the fucking man and working for him is an honor.

When I reached a complete dead end with My Boss, he was the person I went to for advice. I felt bad for thinking of leaving the company because he brought me in, but I didn't know what else to do after continuing to ask for more responsibilities and continuing to receive 'no's. I was not asking for a title promotion. I was not asking for a raise. I just wanted higher-level work. If I were my own employee, I would adopt myself for being ambitiously amazing. After receiving his promise to not get involved, I asked him what I should do to move forward. He advised that if there were higher-level functions I specifically wanted to acquire, then find a way to learn them on my own. And so I did.

I walked over to My BFF and told her what he recommended. She was the only person I could learn from, so I needed to shadow her role in order to master the functions. Thankfully, she was more than happy to assist. Every day, I would arrive to work early, finish my tasks promptly, so that

I could learn how to excel in this position. I also learned that the only person who is going to look out for you is yourself and the only person who can change your fate is also, yourself. So, if I choose not to do anything, I would be more to blame than My Boss.

My second year review meeting was the last puzzle piece to my game plan. It was a hidden test to see how My Boss would react, which would determine how long I'd be willing to stay here. In these serious scenarios I always choose to wear black. Black looks slimming. Black hides nervous sweat stains. Black is intimidating. New Yorkers wear black. My nail polish, also almost black. I was not playing around.

I pulled out the chair from under the table and basked in my glory while she began my review. She boasted of my greatness and had not one note of constructive criticism, besides that I needed to slow down. I'm sorry, I didn't know being fast and efficient was a negative attribute in the workplace. We all know when everyone's work is piled on you there is one deadline when they want things finished. Yesterday.

I sneered, I nodded, I sipped my iced coffee. That remark didn't affect what I was here for. I was here to ask one last time to be a manager and if that was not a possibility, I was out of here.

"Is there anything you would like to add?" she asks.

"There is," I reply. I put down my coffee letting the condensation of my cup sweat down the table. I recline in the chair with my arms crossed like the Godfather to be. "This question becomes more frequent as time passes that you could probably predict what I am going to ask. What do I have to do to secure the position as a project manager? I already know every part of the process and I want the opportunity to achieve it hands on."

She places her hands on her lap and grins as if she is about to tell a child 'that's enough TV watching for the day'. "I think you are just too young for this position," she answers.

Am I also too short? Am I also too pale? Do I also have too many freckles? What else can I not change that is a problem? I have received my last rejection in this place and, I decide, I have absolutely nothing more to lose. "What exactly makes me so young? Is it my work ethic, or the amount of work I am able to take on for others in this company? Or the assistance every department wants from me, offered without my volunteering until email requests flood my inbox? If I'm so young, why would I be trusted with all that responsibility?" I ask.

"No, no it is not your work ethic. I just told you, you are a great asset to our department. Your hard work is critically valued here. When I say you are too young… it is nothing to take personally. Your voice is high toned on the phone. When managers see you they will think you are five years younger than you are. We need our employees to be taken seriously in this position and I don't think hotel managers will because of your age," she answers, reservedly. "Why are you trying to grow so quickly?" she asks.

"I'm starting my third year here. Based on my progression it seems to be the logical next step. I thought wanting to grow was a positive thing. Is it not?" I inquire.

"We need someone to occupy your position and you do an impeccable job at it. We will let you know when we feel is the right time," she confirms.

When is the right time, when I am thirty? I don't think so. "Ok. Just so I can be 100% clear about this… there is definitely no room for growth here?" I ask one last time with my ears opened to receive her response.

"Sadly, that is correct. We are just too small of a company and I would like someone your senior to fill that higher position," she answers.

"Ok. That is all I need to know," I smile, "thank you for your time, and the raise. I accept." I get up from the chair, smear my wet coffee cup across the table leaking onto the floor and shut the door behind me. I pelt my cup in the trash and walk straight to My BFF's office trying to keep a low heat on my frustration.

My age. My age! One thing I could not change. I was proud of my age. I was proud of what I had accomplished thus far and she shit all over it. I sat in My BFF's office and vented my entire review. She was in shock, thinking the result was ridiculous, inequitable, and uncalled for. I agreed. I asked *four* times to be a manager and received *four* no's. The only positive I could take from this was that I never gave up in asking for what I wanted.

What more could I have done? I don't think anything. Could I have gone above her head? I could of. But that is not how I operate. At least I can say I learned everything I wanted if the position were my own. I asked my mentors for advice and I carried it out. I exhausted all of my options. I am no longer the one to blame anymore.

My BFF met with My Boss for their weekly meeting and expressed to her my concerns, even though I never asked her to. Either way I didn't care. It was a dead end from here. She explained to My Boss that due to lack of opportunity and ability to grow, I was planning on leaving the company, which would be a huge loss for everyone. My Boss didn't believe her initially until she started reading off my lists of projects. After realizing what she was losing, she voiced utter shock and disappointment that I was really considering to leave. She expressed to My BFF that she would give me whatever I wanted to stay, but I didn't believe one word of that *mishigas*.

The real loss was that I actually wanted to stay in this company. I would have been happy to work for ten more years like everyone else, if that option was available. But one can only take so much discouragement and oversight in a workplace that halts you at every turn. How many times do you need to ask, until you're completely run dry? Well, I guess I can answer that. *Four* times.

She called me back into her office to discuss the matter of quitting. I knew what I was going to hear when I walked through that door, but I still had a 10% chance of hope left in my faith bank. I don't know why she acted like it was a surprise. You commend me for my greatness yet insult my physiognomies?

Age does not predicate performance. She claimed that if she were to allow me to be a project manager, there would be no one to help me with the two and a half jobs I am currently doing now, plus the project management job I was about to take on.

I knew this was a fucked up scenario, but if it were the only way to get what I wanted and earned, I was willing to have an overwhelming year of death for the hands on experience. Little did she know, I already trained myself on everything she would have to train me, so I was fully prepared to prove her wrong.

THE NOVICE STAGE

I will never forget my first day of work when My Boss lectured me on office rules. "Because you are young and this is your first job, I am going to review with you our guidelines," she began.

Rule #1: If you need to use the bathroom during the day, make sure you arrive early or stay late, in order to make up the time. – Not a joke.

Rule #2: Guests are not allowed in the office at any time.

Rule #3: Lunch breaks are optional.

Lunch breaks are optional? In what world would lunch ever be an option? Any meal of the day is beyond mandatory in the rules of life. Optional is a word for spicy or no spicy on your falafel pita. Not about the entire meal!

When new employees are hired into the company, they are assigned a mentor. On their first day, the mentor takes the new employee out to lunch. This lunch is a trap for the employee, making it seem like every day is full of rainbows, when actually, tomorrow would be dark and full of terrors. The mentors pretend there is no such thing as terror, until the next day arrives and they find out for themselves. Surprise! You just entered the gates of hell. Good luck.

I was assigned to be the mentor of a new hire who was my age. Not sure My Boss could handle this much youth in one area. The day I took her out to lunch I didn't know how to answer her questions.

"Where do you guys go out to eat around here?" she asked.

"Ehh…" I searched for words.

"Do you guys ever go out to eat together?" she asked.

"Ehh…" I searched for more empty words.

"Do you guys ever do happy hour?" she asked.

"EHHHHH….." I exploded.

The response I wanted to give: If you are not eating meals chained to your desk with your eyes glued to your monitor, you clearly don't have enough work to do. Also, you can't go to the bathroom. But enjoy working here!

I'll never forget the early days when My Boss would walk across the office, interrupting me mid-bite so we could regroup for the day. She could clearly see in plain sight that I was about to fuel my extreme state of hunger, and I would drop my fork, unplug my computer, to then sit in her dungeon for five hours straight. No, somehow I didn't lose weight. Yes, I wish it only were that easy. But once I slowly went through occupational puberty and turned into a wo-man, I learned to start saying one of the first words we learn as toddlers. "No."

The intimidation factor is increasingly high at your first big girl job. You constantly want to do your best and let your work outshine itself. With all of that pressure, it's easy to forget to take care of yourself. I completely missed that part at orientation. Just kidding there is no orientation at your first job. This isn't school. This is Module 1: Introduction to Real Fucking Life, kids.

The moment I realized my hands were in every department and that the small piles were turning into large piles upon my shoulders, I discovered the power: none of this would get done without me. Therefore, from here on out, everything will be done on my time, when I say, and in the order that I desire. Why? Because even though I was Santa's favorite helper, I was pretty damn important.

They needed me more than I needed them. When I wanted to go to the bathroom, I went, because I am fucking human and should be allowed to pee whenever I want. When asked to meet pre first-bite or in the midst of lunch, my response remained a big fat no. I needed my time to feed my fat.

As novices in the business world, we need to learn to stick up for ourselves and what we believe is right. Working hard is required. In this world, people have made it a choice. It is not. You must pay your dues. Show your worth. And show yourself, most of all, what you can accomplish. No one can be prouder of your own accomplishments than yourself.

The first mistake we learn is letting people take advantage of us because we're young. We don't even realize it's happening until we're trapped in the black hole and can't get out. Being fearful of letting someone down, opening the floor to rejection from a question, not building yourself back up from a mistake are all the faults we make in the novice stage. Life consists of trial and error. You try, or you don't, but wouldn't you rather try than not at all? Not trying is already a born failure. The error is worth making if you end up growing from it. Trial and error is how I grew out of the novice stage.

I was right (*slow eye blink, smile*). I WAS important. The moment My Boss realized this little birdy was going to fly away was when I got everything I wanted. Well, not everything. I should have asked for the buffet. I accidently ordered à la carte. The manager position was earned and I was proving her wrong left and right.

My first assignment was to research hotels in New York, Los Angeles, Orlando, and Chicago for meeting spaces. My Boss tried to discourage me, saying that this task would take one month to complete and that the managers on the other line would not take me seriously once they detected my youthful tone. The only way I was allowed to make these calls was if she could sit in an office with me and "critique my voice and word selection." Too bad she couldn't make it that day. Two hours later (pee breaks included), I had already made calls to all four cities, outlined notes for each hotel, disclosed available and unavailable dates, and had proposals from each city printed in hand. Adding another gold star to my winning streak may have issued her another heart attack in the *proved you wrong* category.

I accomplished everything I wanted to over the next couple of months. I was only keeping afloat with my workload, but the rewards I attained through being a manager fulfilled my previous professional void completely. I loved learning and I loved being hands on. Being little and fierce looked good on me. Everything I was trained to do I carried out on-site. I learned more about myself through every challenge, every hiccup, and every solution.

I held my work to a certain standard. My performance was a reflection of myself. I worked with individuals who would constantly drop the ball and that, in turn, would affect how my performance was examined. I was constantly, 24/7, trying to prove that they did not make a mistake in giving me this opportunity. That any youngen recruited next in line would be given the chance because I helped pave the way for them. I wanted to make a difference not just for myself and in this company, but to set a standard for all perspectives that age should not be discriminated against. Work ethic and drive are the only things that should be judged. My work wasn't just an A+. It had to be an A+++ because in a blink of an eye it could all be taken away and I will never be given that chance again.

Sometimes there are factors that we can't control, but we still have to be accountable for them. My Boss used to tell me my weakness was delegating responsibility. I disagree. Since we were understaffed it was common to hire temporary staff at each location we worked. We requested that our hired staff would be held to a certain standard of intelligence, but that doesn't mean that we were going to get it. My Boss didn't want to pay the higher rate for qualified staff even though we pleaded we needed it.

One woman got her "monthly gift" and dramatically made an exit. Others fell asleep on the job or were afraid of human contact. Some exerted too much human contact. Others wore workout clothes to high-level dinner meetings, and some were over seventy-five years old and technology wasn't their forte. Long story short, you get what you pay for and sometimes, you really can only rely on yourself.

For me, delegating responsibility is the most basic instruction. But when I know the game is in overtime and I can physically do something 5x faster in the time that it would take to explain it, I do it myself. Why? Because my name is on it. It is my meeting. It is my responsibility and these temporary staff hires fall under my reign. One fuck up and it's not on them, it's not on production, and it's not on the hotel. It's on me. And because I am very aware of where the blame will fall, relying on them was not a risk I was willing to take. I didn't see this as a weakness. I saw it as strength. My strength of possessing tunnel vision of only choosing to succeed and that there was no other option but to finish the race in time. Delegating responsibility is easy. But for me, doing it myself was easier.

I was never the type to ask for help because I knew everyone has their own job to do. I didn't want to bother my colleagues asking to help me move 100+ pound cases, sky high boxes from one room to the other because I knew, in time, I could do it on my own. It would take me two decades to get there, but, in the end, I knew I could do it. Help would be wonderful, but still, I never asked. The only time I would ask for help was if I desperately needed it. This was mostly never, but tonight, I was desperate.

Our meeting in Texas adjourned at 10:00 PM as hundreds of participants walked out the door. Once the last attendee left, the production team and I started to tear down the room. At this time, some employees were done or had to finish up their own job. The only difference was they had an entire team of people to assist them. I didn't.

I had too much to do and no one to help me. As I saw the rush of my coworkers run to the bar, I called out one simple question, "Wait! Can you guys please help me for five minutes?"

"Nope!" they echoed as they descended down the escalators.

I turn around looking over all the shit I have to pack, organize and ship in large pelican boxes that could fit multiple dead bodies inside. Cases and more shit in the room to my right. Cases and more shit in the main ballroom and to my left. Three meeting rooms and a foyer I had to pack up all, by, myself. I press my hands deep over my eye sockets until I wipe the frustrating tears off my face. Two years, five months and eight cities later, I finally hit my breaking point.

This is when I realized that the job was way too much physical labor for one person. This is when I asked myself, how did I last so long doing all of this on my own? This is when I noticed I was everyone's aid but had none of my own. This is when I understood, that I was being taking advantage of and this is when I started to question if it was because of my age.

My Boss hasn't traveled to a meeting since I started in the position. She has no idea the scale of what set up and teardown consists of for one person. Regularly, My BFF would be my other helping hand but she had fallen ill from our continued travels. I sent her to her room hours before the meeting ended, offering to cover for her, thinking I would be able to handle every position at one time. Now I sit here, carrying an entire department with no one to be my support when I need it most.

Three hours later, I finished the job leaving salty rivers of footsteps behind. I cried all the way up to my room until I called my mom in panic attack mode. I may have also been PMSing at the time because this breakdown was a full-blown natural disaster that would not dissipate. She waited while I calmed down and reminded me that it's over now. Everything will be okay, breathe.

I could hear my dad in the background shouting, "Who cares! Fuck them." With his outburst on repetition, it hit me. That was my problem. I cared. I was the only one who truly cared about succeeding in my job. I cared about the success of the show in its entirety and the relationships with my colleagues who I viewed as family. For caring too much, I was left in the dust to take this whole aftereffect very personally. It was personal to me because it involved me. I personally needed the help. If anyone needed me, I was there. I acted in all things with love through life and when my job was hit, so was my heart.

I was always aware of the saying, *"Don't take it personally, it's just business,"* but I could never believe that side of corporate culture. When it involves a person, it's personal. Good business comes from good relationships and you don't have that without a connection.

I returned home with the full decision in my mind to resign. I was not putting any additional practice time in the game when my losing record was already 1-10. Returning home, I was mentally defeated. Returning to the office, I was depleted. I had to prepare for our department debrief to discuss the meeting's pros and cons. I debated with myself on whether I wanted to expose my frustrations to My Boss if I was planning to leave anyway. Then, I realized not speaking up weighed less than vocalizing my concerns. So, I decided to tell her, because either way, I was on my way out.

I explained the situation of the deserted desert I was stranded in and how I felt about it. I pressed play on the cause, effect, and solution of my professional, yet frustrating position. I wanted to see if she would be able to offer or create a future resolution. She had nothing to propose. Just ill advice of what I already knew, not to take anything personally.

I disagreed. I had a solution configured for all aspects of the job. I just needed a small army of physical bodies to carry out the tasks. Nothing more. I was not intoning the overwhelming state of my job at hand. I was voicing that our department consists of one person and how was one person going to carry an entire department? Somehow, she translated this into a completely different philology. I could sense that she was holding on to this grenade for a while, and she took it out of her ammunition tank at the wrong time in the wrong battlefield, my battlefield.

"If you feel you need more help with your workload, maybe you should come in earlier or leave later. Better yet, give up that weekly spin class."

Jaw dropped. Oh no she didn't. Give up my weekly spin class? I don't even spin anymore! What does exercise have to do with asking for human allies? Here is an example, if you are throwing a Christmas party where you have to cook, clean, decorate, and host at the same time, wouldn't having Aunt Sandy and Uncle Harvey be more helpful than doing it all by yourself? I'm Jewish and I know it takes an army for a Passover Seder. Recruitment is extremely essential.

With my eyes squinted, ears steaming, and mouth opened wide, all I could think of saying in response was the truth, "First of all, it's called cycling. Second of all, that is not my current preferred choice of fitness." I add.

"I also completely disagree with you. I don't need to put in additional hours in the office since I finish my work effectively and efficiently in the eight hours you pay me for. I don't go on Facebook. I don't shop online. I don't watch movies or listen to music like my older colleagues do under this roof. I come in and sit at that desk every single day to do my work and leave when it's finished. All I asked for was a physical pair of helping hands, not metaphorical, while I'm on-site before and after my temp staff leaves. No one ever had to do this job alone to this extent and I would be the first, and now the last." On that note, I was fuming and removed myself from her office to breathe.

Give up that spin class are you kidding? Could you imagine if she found out that I was actually a group fitness instructor? Besides Equinox being my second home, I have been employed there for almost two years as a side job. Equinox keeps me sane by helping me end my day empowered, motivated, and challenged to be at a place I love most. I may not be the thinnest or the strongest, but Equinox is more to me than just a gym. It is what keeps my life balanced.

I came up with a new method of staying afloat. It would be the opposite of how I instinctually operate but it was the only way for me to survive the next six months. I would have to inherit a "*do less, care less*" mentality. If I take a step back and only manage what I feel I can healthily handle, say no to those who I know can do their own work, and rewire my brain to not care about the unimportant stresses of this workplace, I would be able to endure.

Now that I have practiced this mental reverse, it felt so freeing. It's so hard to shift perspective and prompt yourself to take that step back. To remind yourself that your job is not your life. It feels like it's your life because it is what you do and where you spend most of your time, five or more days a week, but check-in with yourself. This is not your life. What you do before and after it, is your life.

I first applied this *"do less, care less"* mentality at our weekly group meeting with My Boss. She may or may not be a working hypochondriac. She stresses about the smallest of issues that I used to take on as being equally as big, make or break, world ending worries. Returning from my 'breaking point' meeting in Texas and preparing for our next show in San Francisco, I listened to how she magnified situations that were never going to take place in real time. Once I realized how insignificant her future stresses were, I couldn't help but breathe a sigh of relief. We were not going to war with North Korea. We were just putting on a little show with big lights and screen projectors. I was taking on all of her anxiety in large quantities thinking if I thought the way she did I would perform at my best. Not anymore. In the grand scheme of things, the world will not end because a post-it note was the wrong color.

As long as you show up, do what you're supposed to do and not the entire carnival act that is your company, you'll be fine. While taking that step back, put yourself first because you are living this life, in this body, and you need to be selfish. Being selfish is not selfish. It's empowering.

During this time of being self-ish, I created a back up plan for my future. With the time I now developed in my schedule for not doing 'other people's work', I decided to find more work for myself. Equinox was already my first plan slash happy pill feeding my existence. But sometimes one back up plan isn't enough and you need to search the sand for others.

During my work trip to San Francisco, I met up with my best friend, Yves, who recently became the lead software designer at a startup. This startup was a designing a new shopping app and they were looking for freelance stylist curators to build product catalogues. I was intrigued. She gave me the opportunity to complete test projects for the company and I instantly formed an addiction to the work, and the rewarded compensation. Since both parties were pleased, they offered me a short contract and I happily accepted. I signed a five-month independent contract not only working two jobs, but now a third. It was difficult waking up super early to work on the deliverables, to then head to my full-time hellhole job, to then teach or work out at Equinox, and continue to work on the startup before bed. You are correct; I was skinny during this time. But without much sleep or free time, I was exhausted. My bank account, however, was not. I may not have believed in the company since the CEO could not see the flaws that were developing in his marque, but I was keeping my eyes on the prize, delivering the assigned work, getting paid, and saving it all for my future plan.

Thinking about the future was a scary subject for me. If My Boss had helped me tread water in my job instead of guiding me towards the sinkhole, I would have maybe stayed for the rest of time. I unfortunately acquired such a hatred working for My Boss, that I was not looking to apply for other full time journeys because I couldn't imagine working for another human being. I didn't even think of working for myself at the time because I didn't know what I wanted to do next. Leaving meant my options were endless. But just like at a frozen yogurt shop, having one hundred toppings to pick from doesn't make your top choices any easier. What I did know is that whatever I decide to do post inferno, I need to make sure I have excess money in my account to make a plan and never look back.

One month after carrying multiple careers, a life changing opportunity was proposed to me. My other best friend, Michelle, was living in London and dating the loveliest Brit I've ever met, Josh. Just so you know, I have a killer English accent and London happens to be my favorite city in the world. I visited London once before and fell in love at first sight with the royal country. Josh and Michelle offered me the chance to come live in London. What a dream! But I did not think it could ever and would ever be possible. I also could not see myself leaving my life to live in another country, *just because*. Yet, it was not *just because* anymore. I needed a new perspective and unfound inspiration for my next step in employment and in life. Everything happens for a reason, and if I could make this work, this could be a once in a lifetime experience.

I can't help but to think how, a few months ago, I was planning to move somewhere for a man. Now, I have another chance to move somewhere, this time for me. And in London! My preferred location before meeting Mr. GQ. And so I accepted. I accepted the challenge of "*why not*?" when I always apprehended the automatic answer "because."

"Why can't I have chocolate?" – "Because."

"Why can't I go outside?" – "Because."

"Why can't I move to another country? – "Because," My parents would often say. But guess who is in control of my life? I am. Guess who decides if I should stay or I should go? I do. Why? "*Because, I said so.*"

Waiting out these next few months to quit, the thought of it was still scary. Leaving home was scary. Walking into the unknown was scary. But I've never been scared before because I've always played it safe. With planning this relocation into a transitional period of exploration, I wasn't prepared. But I was ready. I was ready to explore this new place and my new self. I needed to find a new self because I was not happy with my present being. But if London was calling, and I answered the phone, I would move onward with the intention. Not only because London was a dream, but also because they have an Equinox there, so it was really a no brainer to commit.

As Equinox would say, "Commit to Something."

The Medium

All jokes aside, the thought of quitting was not fun or exciting. It was pretty petrifying. Each passing month counting down to my departure I was scared shitless, pondering if I was making the right decision. Quitting your job is a big fucking deal, especially in this economy and new world we live in. Would this be something I would regret? The reasons why I wanted to leave were credible, but thinking of my day-to-day, primary income, bills, and the thought of working for a new company where I would have to inherit a new work family, made me feel very uneasy. I would have to start completely from scratch.

I felt like I was in limbo. On paper, I had almost everything. In my heart I had absolutely nothing. The same fears that haunted me in Israel were resurfacing and I did not know what to do. I felt like I was finally at the forefront of actually giving everything up because of my root of unhappiness. But how much is happiness worth? After months of debate, I knew it was worth everything. The unknown was scary, but instead of falling into it, I would discover it. I decided I was going to see a Medium.

When I was fifteen years old, I lost one of the most beautiful people in my life. Her name was Robin. She was my nanny. She didn't like when I referred to her as my nanny, she preferred housekeeper, but even though she was the keeper of our house, she was also my keeper, which held a higher title to me. My brother had ADHD growing up and my mom had to focus more attention on him, since he only knew one speed, how to run. While my mom had to keep up with chasing him, Robin stayed behind walking with me. When it was time for her to move on to another family, we could not let her go because she was already threaded into ours. Fortunately for me, I was able to have what felt like two mothers. My mother and Robin. My mom holds the reign of being the best mother in the world. She is selfless, caring, vivacious, and the perfect role model of any super woman in the flesh. I am the mini version of her. She is just taller with blonde hair and a bigger tush. I am so proud of the way she raised me because I am proud of who I have become today. When you are proud of the person you have become, that is when your parents know they have succeeded in the parenting game. Whenever I give birth, I'm dropping my children off to her so she can raise them just like me.

Robin raised me equally to my mother. I will never forget that Sunday, on January 28th, when my mother came into my room to tell me that she had passed away. I remember the look on her face as she opened my door and walked around the side of my bed. "Who died?" I asked her, as the tragedy that occurred was written all over her face. I didn't know until later that my mom found out the news hours before she fed me breakfast, knowing I would not be able to eat for the next couple of days. She was right, and she was incredibly strong. How do you tell your fifteen year-old that her second mother had passed away in her sleep? There is not a day that goes by that I do not think about Robin. When I sat in that park behind my house yelling at God about my first potential job falling through, I'll admit, I was shouting at her too because I knew she was the one protecting me. It took me a while to realize that she was, indeed, my guardian angel. With the course of events taking place after that moment, I discovered that she had helped guide me on the path I was supposed to be on, and with the unknown, I know she will help guide me now.

I have always believed in the supernatural powers of Mediums. Many people don't, but I do. Yes, I watch the shows Long Island Medium and The Hollywood Medium Tyler Henry. Yes, I wrote to their websites to book an appointment and am still waiting for a response. I always wanted to meet with a Medium ever since I was introduced to these shows. Originally, I always wanted to go to reach my Robin, but now, I also wanted to go for myself.

I believe that when I find random pennies on the floor, Robin is placing them in my footpath. I believe when she appears in the storyline of my dreams it is not a coincidence, it is a visitation. Everyone in this world has had someone close to them who has passed away. If you had the slightest chance of speaking to them one last time, would you? Don't lie. We all would. My mentality was, whether I heard from Robin, or not, whether I was told a glimpse of my future, or not, at least I can say to myself that I tried instead of not trying at all. What did I have to lose by seeing a Medium? $150.00, but in the grand scheme of things it was something I always wanted to do…so I did it.

I waited ten years to speak with Robin, and if this Medium could provide the slightest bit of insight on my next endeavor, or give me that push I so desperately yearned for, the interaction would be worth it. I was referred to this Medium by a family friend who had a reading because she could not close the mourning of her late husband. As much as she tried to gather up her emotional pieces on her own, she was unsuccessful and didn't know how to move forward. Prior to the reading she was very skeptical. Since she knew this would not help bring her husband back, she thought what is the point of even going? Now, she confesses it has forever changed her perspective on life after the hard passing of her soul mate. She shared that the specifics of her life, the descriptions of items in her house, and the current and future circumstances of her children could not be known to this Medium. Yet, without ever meeting her before, the Medium was able to uncover it all.

It took me five months to build the courage to finally book an appointment. Prior to this I didn't think meeting with her was necessary (I was waiting for Tyler Henry, to be honest). But, Tyler never called and neither did Teresa Caputo, so I texted this Medium.

I wanted to meet with her for two reasons: to hopefully speak with Robin and to get a glimpse of my future, to answer my ultimate question, will I be okay? Again, I knew I was making the right decision in my life to quit my job, but I needed someone to physically push me out the door to get there. You can only bring yourself so far until you reach the cliff. To jump or not to jump? That is the question. I think the one thing I was most nervous about was not that I didn't have enough money to support myself; I purposely saved for this. Thankfully, living at home for three years, I was able to save and invest the amounts I would be flushing down the toilet paying rent, into the market. I miserably drove my nice car over an hour to and from work, five days a week, to be able figure out my next move without panic. I was afraid to start looking and interviewing to find another job. After working three jobs right now, I honestly didn't want to work anymore. But that was also impossible and not realistic.

I anxiously crossed off each day in my calendar until the day finally arrived. It was here. I planned to head down to meet her after work in Downtown Miami. She chose to meet at a Starbucks, one I have not been to before. In typical Medium fashion, this meeting location was very unusual. Most of the Medium shows I religiously watch meet at a house or quiet place so they can concentrate on the person's energy and spirits. But no, I was at a busy ass Starbucks on Biscayne Blvd waiting in a chair for a woman whom I've never met. As a Type-A American, I was naturally on time, most likely early, and she was late. I texted her that I was in the Starbucks and told her what I was wearing, including that my hair was light brown. I waited apprehensively shaking my legs and feet a million miles a minute, not knowing how to control my nerves.

I keep my eyes locked on the door and the clock waiting for her arrival. I shift my gaze from staring at the time to find a tall blonde woman walk through the door. She looks around, I wave and she spots me across the room, "Are you Brittany?" she asks.

"Hi, yes, I just came from work." I answer.

"Don't tell me any more," she signals with her hands, "I want to know nothing about you or it might mess up the reading. Sorry I was late. I was on the phone," she says.

I nodded. I was so nervous, and, for the first time, I shut up.

She buys a bottle of water and leads outside to the outdoor seating.

"Isn't the outside noise going to bother you?" I ask before taking a seat.

"No, the noise calms me actually. I have so many messages at once I don't like when it is too quiet." She places the bottle of water and a pack of cigarettes on the table. "Do you mind if I smoke? This helps me read," she asks.

Great… I thought. Yes, I mind if you smoke, but I would never tell you that. I don't want you to tell me bad shit about my life. "No, it's fine."

All I can think of is that this is a total scam, sitting outside a busy Starbucks, during rush hour, on one of the most high traffic streets in Downtown. She lights up her cigarette and inhales a drag before she begins. She starts to explain how she became a Medium, at what age, and how she filters through messages from the other side. "Now remember, I am not a fortune teller, but I receive messages from my four angels and I will tell you what they say. Keep in mind, my angels are unfiltered so if they curse, so will I, if they tell me things that are not pleasant, I may tell you as well. Is there is anything you don't want to know?" she asks.

"Um… bad things, or like, death." I answer.

"Can you be more specific?" she asks.

"…No." I reply.

"Ok! Let's begin." She has me take out a pen and paper to write down specific notes that I might deem of importance. She downloads multiple messages at once, so as she jumps from one thought to the next she has me write everything down. She goes into detail on how she channels messages from her four angels and spirits. She instructs that I answer a yes or no to her questions or statements, but to not give specifics so she could discover them on her own. And that she did. As promised, she cursed, she told me things I wish I never knew, and things I already knew. I know reading this you are thinking she and I are absolutely crazy, but we're not! Every Medium is different so I keep a very open mind also knowing that if I was closed off, it may throw off my session.

"If you had hundreds of thousands of friends on Facebook, that is how many spirits you have on the other side. You are a very old soul. You did not live many lives, but you are old," she begins.

I always felt like an old soul. "Thank you." What else was I going to say? I sit in my chair, unable to stop fidgeting while the backs of my legs were sticking to the uncomfortable patio chair. I would definitely have line indentations after this reading is over.

I listened and I took notes, but I didn't automatically believe every word she said. I made it a point to challenge each message I disagreed with. I still wasn't sure she was the real deal. This reading was nothing but a bed of daisies as portrayed in the TV shows, but three hours later we touched on very valid points of my life, my future, and finally, Robin.

There is one thing the Medium did admit. Besides not being a fortuneteller, since she also knew nothing about the background of my life or my last name, she could not differentiate accurately between past, present and future. I would have to help decipher that on my own.

PAST

"Are you interested in knowing about any future or past lovers?"

"Sure," I said. OF COURSE I AM. I was aware that the relationship part of my life was slim, so I was curious what hoopla or truth she would come up with. She takes a drag of her cigarette and sips a drink of water.

"Who is the Jewish guy?" she asks.

"Which one?" I ask in return.

"Don't tell me, hold on…" She takes another inhale of smoke and looks in the direction of the road, "He doesn't live here. He lives in another country. He's gorgeous and tall. Oh, he's very good looking, good for you," she winks, "Is he in the army or something?"

I leaned forward and my mouth dropped. "What did you just say?" I ask.

"His name starts with an M or something, you loved him, wow, but it wasn't realistic. Are you planning on seeing him again?" she asks.

"WAIT… what! How do you even know this?" I ask her.

"What a shame. You really loved him. He loved you too, I could tell, but it was never going to work. Your lives are too different. He was jealous of you," she says.

"Jealous of me? How could he possibly be jealous of me?" I ask.

"You had your life figured out, he didn't. He still doesn't. He has no idea what he is going to do with his life. You already have yours planned out in your head like a timeline on the wall." She points in the air. "He envied that part of you and it made him resentful of you," she answers.

I sat back in the chair and looked up. What the fuck? Was this true? How did she tap into all of this, especially him!

"I know he knocked your socks off but it won't end well with you. Also, your spirits don't like him so you have to let him go. Sorry. Are you planning on seeing him again or not? Or does no one know you are thinking about this?" she asks.

"I cannot believe you just asked me that. I mean, if I tell you it will ruin the reading. Maybe I'll tell you when it is over but, I spoke to him maybe three days ago and decided I may take a trip to see him if all works out to plan," I tell her.

Three days prior to this reading, I received a text from Mr. GQ. He sent me a picture of us lying in the sand captioned, "Thinking of you." My heart stopped when I saw his name flash across my screen, but once I opened it I began to smile. I asked him how he was, and he told me that work was hard, but he still loved being on the water. I told him I was still planning to leave my job and my next journey would hopefully lead me to London.

"While you're on this side of the world, maybe you will take a trip to see me," he suggests. I could take a trip to see him…. maybe this is how life wanted it. But if that opportunity came I said I would potentially consider it. I had a lot to accomplish before ever making the option to see him again a priority.

She finishes her cigarette, puts it out, and lights up another, "Just to let you know, if you do see him, it will delay your entire future. So, I advise you not to."

My eyes pop out of my sockets. I cannot believe I was hearing this. Delay my entire future? Is the universe playing against us? I sink back into my chair and pause to take all of this in and breathe. Did I think of taking her advice right then and there?

Absolutely not. But I did keep it in the back of my mind, as I also wasn't sure where my future was going.

"Most importantly, your heart chakra is completely closed off. We need to open it," she instructs.

"That's funny. I know it is, but I don't care to open it." I answer.

"I know you don't care, that is the problem. Your chakras are totally imbalanced. Someone breaks your heart and you close it right back up to focus on you and only you. Your first love is also to blame. He damaged you so badly your heart was closed off for four years....does that make sense?" she asks.

"No," I answer. My first, real love was Mr. GQ and only a couple of months have passed since then.

"He has a brother and a sister. His parents are divorced..." she continues.

Mr. GQ's parents are not divorced and he has two brothers, so this makes no sense. "Um...no."

"Well, then they are living two totally different lives," she laughs, "Are you sure? Think again. It is not the army boy, stop thinking that."

I try to think about who my first love could be and I all I can think of is him, "I really don't know."

She shakes her head left and right, "He has a name but he goes by another name, who is that?"

I think really hard. I start calling out random names, "Bernie, Bernard? Benny, Benjamin? I really don't know."

"No, listen… I have this friend named Chris, but we call him Cairo as a nickname. Everyone calls him Cairo, but his name is Chris. Does that make sense?"

"Not really," I say.

"This happened six years ago," she affirms.

Six years, ago, six years ago… I think back and realize, I am an idiot. My high school boyfriend! We called him only by his last name, not his first name! That must be him. I say his name out loud and she cries out, "Yes! Thank you. You are making me think I am crazy."

"Oh my gosh! I am so sorry. I was a teenager so I completely forgot about it," I react.

"Good, he deserved to be forgotten about, but that was your first love so that we are clear," she says.

"Yes, we are clear. I just thought after being with the Israeli, he was the first time I felt real love. My high school boyfriend and I don't even speak. I honestly never thought he damaged me. That's interesting," I realize.

Before my high school boyfriend became my first love, he was first, my best friend. I loved him dearly as a person and the relationship grew into something greater. Six months later, his parents got a divorce. He experienced an extremely tough time, being the oldest of three kids. Even when he was not strong, he always had to act like he was. With these whirlwinds of emotion pushed all the way down into his body, his rage capsulated at high speed aimed right for my direction. Even though I didn't deserve it, I took all of the heat because I couldn't imagine what he was going through. But most importantly, I just wanted to be there for him. Then I finally came to terms that being there was not going to be enough. After almost a year of degradation, I was done with the hurt, shame, and embarrassment he internally and publicly brought upon me.

I could be experiencing the best day of my life, and one small act of his unkindness would ruin it. One second, one hurtful word, or no words at all, was all it would take to destroy my twenty-four hours of internal sunshine. So looking back, maybe he did damage me. But it also cured me. Because from that day forward, during that period in time, I learned to love myself and put myself first. I realized I changed completely, for him. I changed my needs, wants, and focus to become completely available for him, but completely unavailable to my friends. I would always leave a window of opportunity just to see him, even if for only five minutes. It needed to end not just for us, but also for me, to recognize my self-worth that I increasingly lost along the way.

Now, I am single - and I am hella proud of it. I am my proudest self with no one to answer to, and no one to ruin my day. I can have one hundred splendid days in a row because I am in control of them. I know that I am important and I love my life in its complete entirety. Having a man in your life should be an addition to your happiness, not the sole reason for the opposite. It took me a while to rewire that mentality post breakup. But you have to remind yourself; the only person who can make your life abundant is yourself. Maybe the Medium is right. Maybe he did damage me. But the real magic lies when something is damaged, it can be repaired. And because of that repair I learned the most important lesson of all: to love myself.

She continued, "Most importantly, don't ever settle. I can sense you're picky, but that is okay. Don't ever let someone tell you it's not. Life is not worth settling for, so why should your love life be any different?"

"I always thought I was going to settle," I tell her.

"Don't ever settle, because if you settle and you get married, you will get a divorce," she instills.

WOAH THERE. Pump the breaks. Not cool, but noted.

"Do you want to know who you are going to marry?" she asks.

"Oh my god, do you know who?" I ask in caution.

"Yes," she answers.

Oh my god, did I want to know? No. Because if I did, that ruins the spontaneity of life! I always felt like I could not see myself marrying a stranger. I always felt that it would be someone I already knew. But I didn't want to know who it was. So out of curiosity, I only asked for clues.

"Do I know him?" I ask.

"Yes," she answers.

"Do I like him?" I ask.

She laughs, "That will be entirely up to you. I do know that his parents are divorced. He wears suits every day to work and when he is home he is in loungewear attire. You guys work. He does his thing, you do yours, and he's fine with that. Just keep in mind, he does not have the perfect body you are looking for."

"What do you mean? Is he fat?" I ask.

"He's not fat, he's just not perfect. And he has scruff on his face," she confirms.

"Ugh, these are like all the things I don't look for in a guy," puzzled.

"Well maybe your taste will change," she jokes.

"Maybe." I have a feeling that I know who this person is, and I am not sure in this moment that I am okay with that or see it happening. But hey, it may not all be bad. In the end, only God knows. Oh, and the Medium.

PRESENT

She dives into the occupational aspects of my life, unable to distinguish what is in the past, present, or future. She does not know my age or what I do for a living. Even though I told her I just left work, she could think I work at a local smoothie shop, manning the cashier after high school. I do after all look borderline seventeen.

Through her messages she predicted that I would, or am currently, working for a company that has me traveling all over the United States. With traveling, Miami would always be my home base. This, I knew, was the job I had now. She projected that I would have an opportunity to work for a company in California, maybe LA, related to an e-commerce platform resembling Amazon. I was also already doing this for the shopping app with Yves, but out of San Francisco.

"Who's Josh?" she asks.

"What?" I ask.

"Josh. I see his name with an asterisk next to it. Write it down. I don't know what that means but we'll come back to it."

All I could think of was Josh, Michelle's boyfriend. I don't know how he would come into my reading.

"Also write down the number six. I see the number six correlate with Josh. Does that make sense?" she asks.

A light bulb went off again! Josh invested in a six-bedroom property in London where I would live if I decide to hop over the pond. Maybe she was seeing it playing out into the future. "Yes, this makes sense."

"Great. Well with that said, you are about to have a major transition coming up in your career," she confirms.

FUTURE

A major transition. This is exactly what I was waiting to hear. This would be the push that I needed to get out of the company and move on to the next endeavor.

"You will have two transitions coming up that I can see. The first will be this summer, the most important. You will be making a huge move but it will not last long. Your transition will begin in the summer and have a milestone in the end of September where you will begin a new career path. You will need to be patient because it will take almost two years to reach the success it was made to. In the meantime, you will work hard on it and it will not be financially rewarding until it is finished."

I did not ask her what the project would be since I felt that if I asked, I would be cheating the game of life. She also asked me if I was twenty-eight years old (which we know I'm not), because she predicted I would be having another transition at that age. I used to always think that was the age when I was probably going to be in a serious relationship or get engaged. Twenty-eight was the age where I felt I would be most comfortable and confident enough to give myself to another. Maybe the universe caught onto that and delivered the message to her.

I always believed marriage would be an afterthought next to my steady career, and she told me not to worry about my biological clock ticking because if I want to have kids later, I can. I have no idea why people my age and younger are deciding to wed. What is the rush? You know what happens after marriage? Babies. A twenty-five year old is not ready for a baby! You are still a baby. Who makes your doctors appointments – you or your mom? Probably your mom. We are still in the period of figuring out our lives and who we are as people. Finding our purpose and committing to our being doesn't happen overnight. It takes years of doing and reflecting.

I believe that your twenties are supposed to be **yours**. All about you, for ten whole years. You go to college. You land your first job. Then it is the trial and error period of adulthood for ten more years. Until you're hopefully ready to get your shit together, you glue it until it's solid. It is the span of time where you really learn about yourself before life really sets in. Once you hit thirty, and thirty is a great age (until wrinkles start to crease), you should save the twenties for getting to know yourself. Know what you like and don't like. Find out what real fear means to you. Experience happiness and sadness, gain and loss. This is the time to challenge yourself and guide your own light.

I am ready to follow that light. As we explore my future path, I realize two hours have passed and Robin has yet to appear in my reading. "Wait, I have someone really important I want to come through and she hasn't yet. Why is that?" I ask.

She tells me that some spirits who are content on the other side don't necessary feel the need to come through. I would not take that for an answer. I waited ten years for this! In the case of an absent spirit, she asked to bring pictures of loved ones if they didn't come forward, so she could bring them forth. I take out the only picture of Robin I could find. Before I show it to her, she asks me to turn it upside down so that she cannot see the actual photo. She takes the picture and flattens it in-between her hands. She closes her eyes and a part of me feels like I'm at a magic show, but I patiently wait while internally yelling at Robin that she better come talk to me, or else.

Based on the Medium TV shows I watch, I expect Robin's spirit to enter gracefully with warm hugs and kisses. But this is not a TV show and that forecast was far from the truth. Instead, Robin ascended in the physical form she passed away in. Sometimes, spirits who have passed take the form of their younger self, current self, or the self they were most happy with before they passed. I anticipated that she would tell me how much she loved me, how much she missed me, and how proud of me she was. She ended up telling nothing of that sort. She expressed moments in her life from her early years as a little girl, to now. The Medium warned me that spirits are unfiltered and even if there were things I should not know, they were going to tell her, who would, in turn, tell me anyway. The Medium relays that Robin is telling her stories about my family, growing up with us, and then gushed how much she loved my brother and how much she loved me. She referred to me as her baby. That was all I needed to hear.

Besides loving me, she was still protective over me, which led to how unhappy and unsupportive she was of my relationship with the Israeli. LOL, awkward. Spirits know everything. I was shocked that out of all the things in the world to tell me, she would bring that up! "Stay away from that boy, now," the Medium uttered in Robin's voice. I looked at her and laughed, because this is not the first time I heard this.

I have very vivid dreams and I usually remember each detail when I awake. In one, I was in a park with Mr. GQ lying in the grass, resting face down with my cheek upon my arms. Mr. GQ was sitting next to me placing flowers on my back. When I look up, I see Robin sweeping the grass in front of me. I look at her and grab him, "Oh my God, this is Robin, you have to meet her! She is very important to me," I voiced. As I lift myself from the grass, he starts walking in the opposite direction. She sweeps past me, "Girl, what you doin' with that boy?" and at that moment I realized, uh-oh, she doesn't want me to be with him. Sometimes in my dreams, I have the realization that I know she has passed away. That even though the dream feels real, I know this is her spirit visiting me. I wanted them to meet each other, but he walked away, and there I stood with Robin. I should have known when I woke up what that would have meant, but maybe I didn't want to listen to what my subconscious was trying to tell me.

Was this the beautiful, fulfilling reading that I wanted from who I felt was my second mother? No. But, she will always be my nurturing, guardian spirit close to me for the rest of my life. Would I ever recommend others to see a Medium? Yes, but only if that person feels the need for a specific purpose or significance. If not, it is not necessary to see one. Some of my friends want to have a reading just to see what the Medium will say, but I recommend going only if you have an instinctual desire to reveal bare deliberations. I yearned for guidance. I needed a push into the direction I wanted to go, but again, I was scared. We all live in fear some way or another and I felt that I was at the tip of my peak. All I needed was the universe to tell me, take that fucking leap, you'll be okay. And when I did, I never looked back.

I walked into this reading with doubt, and walked away with a basket full of clarity. I sat in the driver's seat of my car without turning on the engine. I reclined my seat and opened the sunroof shade to look out into the stars while downloading these large pieces of validation. Validating that maybe Mr. GQ is not the right man for me, like I thought. That maybe he is supposed to be the man who taught me how I should be loved and treated. Validating that my job does not serve me. That it is an anchor in my path that is stopping my ship from sailing onward. That the not thought possible is possible, reaching my goal to move overseas by twenty-five years old. Whether it is for a short time or a long time, the transition was coming. Ready or not, here I come. I am no longer afraid. I am ready for *change*.

I am now sure that the views and uncertainties of the path I laid out for myself were the right ones. That I wasn't jumping off of it into a new one, I was mending the crack in the road that I almost fell in. Stepping over that line of fear is what helped me hike up that metaphorical mountain. And these are my twenties! These are the times to take that jump, to befriend fear, to live in the right and the wrong, to create mistakes and solutions. I felt I was on the verge of making my own solution. And the view from the bottom was great, but I was more interested in seeing the view from the top. I finally expanded my tunnel, and my vision is now clear.

Resilience

Brexit

Life is full of unsure moments. If there is one thing I was most positively sure of, it was being sure of myself. These unsure moments shape not just who you are going to be, but guide you in the direction of who you will become. Are you going to wait for challenges to befall on you, or are you going to create your own challenges? Unsure moments are bared based on the fact that we cannot tell what the future holds. We feel that we have more to lose than to gain. But who decides that we have more to lose than to gain? You do. And for that reason, I didn't think of this unsure moment as a potential loss from uncertainty. I only saw the outcome as a gain.

The reward, no matter how big or small, would be greater than any achievement thus far because I chose to make it so. Then comes a time when someone asks you, "Are you ready for this?" And after you retort affirmation, "Yes, I am ready to make this move," they ask a second time, "Are you sure?" Instinctually I respond, "I am sure," the real question is, "Why aren't you?"

Months pass and I can't count down fast enough to my final departure. The first week of June was our last conference and I could finally begin to close the door on the past three years in this cycle. My mentality during the hell week of my last conference in Chicago was to repeat to myself, "Self - this is the last time I will finish this specific task. Expire to bed this late in the night. Pack this last of twenty-one cases. Lift this fifty-pound apparatus. Stain my suit pants from crawling on the floor. Scuff my Tory Burch loafers. Suffer from bloody cuts and bruised knees, and most importantly, imperfect my perfectly manicured nails by shredding these newly dehydrated hands." This would be the final marathon of the last spin class My Boss didn't want me to take. Biking up that climb, turning the resistance to the left, and flying down the mountain on the road to liberation.

Before returning to the office, my bones were aching with exhaustion and I spent the weekend buried in the covers. The next day I would have to go back to my desk but I simply did not want to. You realize, out of every employee in the office, I was the only one who was not allowed to work remotely? Was there a particular reason that I did not deserve this privilege of working from home? No, but My Boss simply would not allow it. I was the type of employee that if I were deathly sick, I would have to come into the office just for her to then send me home, after she got proof and agreed.

I always felt I had something to prove. I felt I had to demonstrate to her that the heat radiating off of my body was a fever, or my face was a swollen North Alaskan pale from a sinus infection, so that she would believe I was ill. I would always politely ask permission for things that should not need permission. After the conference in Chicago, I decided I am not going in tomorrow because I should not have to. I should not have to prove my exhaustion in the flesh, or that my sickness is authentic. For the first time, I did not ask. Instead I told her, I was not coming in.

"(no subject)

I am exhausted and I am taking a personal day.

Thanks,

Brittany"

Not only would I never write an email this unprofessional, with no subject line, salutation, or signature that did not include a "Best Regards," I was telling My Boss for the first time what I wanted to do. I am not coming in. This was the day I may or may not have grown a pair of balls. This is the email that shook the volcano that was almost due to erupt.

I always made My BFF aware when I was about to do something and always looked for her approval. She was my voice of reason when I let my emotions take over my mind. I sent her a text that I was not coming in and she agreed that I shouldn't. She was proud of my simple yet meaningful email to My Boss and pretended as if she knew nothing when she was called into the dungeon. My Boss expressed that she felt my email was slightly rude and definitely abnormal coming from me. My Boss needed to know what was wrong.

After every conference we have a debrief meeting reviewing all negative and positive outcomes that took place throughout the symposium. My BFF made all of our obstacles, frustrations, and overwhelming lack of assistance known. Two people cannot do twenty people's jobs. Correction, two people can do twenty people's jobs because she and I did successfully, but not without sweat, tears, and blood boiling enervation.

The next day, I come to the office giving zero fucks. My Boss calls me in to discuss the meeting and my energy is depleted. The tone in my voice could not be more quiet or calm. After knowing, but pretending not to know, what her and my BFF discussed, I expressed my most honest thoughts keeping in the back of my mind my most famous question of the year, "How can this be changed in the future?" After debriefing from beginning to end what shouldn't have taken place, but did as a result of other people's slothfulness in our company, I asked just that, "What is the solution?"

It was like listening to a broken record. I knew how this could change. Hire additional staff to support your team running the entire event because no one can be in three places at once, and I can't clone myself. Do you know how much I would love to clone myself? I wish I knew employees as good and as fast as I am. I offered solutions to My Boss just to see that even though I was planning to quit, would she decide to offer help in any capacity in the future? What did I receive? Another big fat no to add to my collection.

The help I need on-site isn't sending out an email, creating an excel sheet or database. Math was never my forte, but if the SAT question asked, if I have ten cases that weigh one hundred pounds each and I need to move them from the fourth floor, to the lower lobby on the opposite side of the hotel, how many people would I need to help me pack and move them? (I look around… oh, there is just me). That, my friends, isn't complaining, it is just acknowledging an unmanageable task for a 5'3" girl who weighs one hundred and fifteen pounds. Just kidding, I wish I weighed that much but let's pretend on the best day, I do. Knowing that I was quitting, I had nothing to lose if I asked once more. The worst she could say is no - and she did.

Each day went by at sloth speed and I needed to finally pick an end date. I also needed to decide how I was going to do it. My Boss planned to go on vacation for a week and a half, so I figured I would quit when she returned. The summers were slow and my lists of responsibilities were short. This way I could sit back and collect without anyone to bother me.

One thing I knew for sure was that I was heading to London. This was going to be presented as my sole reasoning for resigning. As unhappy as I was at this company, I was still thankful for all that I had learned and experienced. I did not want it to be an immature, unprofessional, parting. I wanted it to be a clean, amicable break up. Since this was my third home (i. Home, ii. Equinox, iii. Work), and I worked with these colleagues more than I saw my own social circles, I felt like I was preparing for a divorce. Needless to say, I knew this would not end well, but if there was any positive divorce to take place in this world, I wanted this to be the first.

I was waiting on Michelle to give me the final go that I officially had a place to stay in London. This was the last piece to my puzzle in securing my game plan and subplot before I quit. If I was planning on doing something this life changing before the deal was closed, I needed to believe it myself first. This is why I didn't mind delaying until after My Boss's vacation because I was waiting until each part was set in stone. Either way, I knew that London was in my future and whenever that day of arrival may be, I was definitely going.

While My Boss is of town, I decided it's time to tell my coworkers. The first one I told was My BFF. I knew it would be hard as she was the apple to my pie, but I needed to take myself out of the oven before my crust burned. I sat down in her office and told her that I had an opportunity to go to London and live in my best friend's boyfriend's humble abode. This was an experience I was offered once before and passed up six months ago. This time, I would not pass it up again.

She knew my frustrations and the constant hurdles I tried to overcome in our company, but despite all of my discussions and desires for growth, this company was not going to be my long-term home. How could you cement a foundation with cracks that wanted to stay broken as long it was still standing? I didn't want to change the way things were done. I just wanted to make it more efficient. I knew that every single person in this company, no matter how much money they made, were extremely unhappy. If they were to take a survey of happiness in the workplace, each employee would fail miserably, with a successful F+ in satisfaction (the + is the effort for taking the survey to begin with).

Telling My BFF first was very difficult. Also because it meant that this was real. I pull my chair up to hers, placing her hands in mine as we weep. I didn't think being this close to someone who was not your family was possible, but she became family to me. The reason I stayed this long in this company was because of her. There is always that one person you overly enjoy working with and she was that person for me, but it got to a point where even her sunlight could not shine through my clouds. I found myself no longer smiling and forcing myself to laugh, that people would ask me "What's wrong?" throughout the day, instead of a usual "Good morning" greeting. This is when I knew this job was significantly affecting me and that nothing was going to resolve my sadness other than leaving.

The worst part about all of this was feeling like I was leaving her. I felt like I was abandoning her and my other close coworkers. At one point I asked myself, was I being selfish because I wasn't just leaving this company, I was leaving them? That is how attached I had become. I then had to remind myself that I am the one in this job and I have to suffer in it, not them. I maxed out my resources and did everything I could to stay but my options ran dry. Even if we could bask in each other's miseries, the difference was that I had a way out and they didn't. Or did they?

I would encourage them time and time again that you are in control of your happiness. Let your happiness overpower the upset in your life. But I found that I wasn't even taking my own advice, until now. The difference was that they had families to provide for and I just had myself. That was the part that wasn't fair for them. But why should someone twice my age not be able to start again or find a new passion within the work field?

I yearned to be excited to get out of bed every morning and go to work. I once felt that way in the novice stage. I knew successfully attaining excitement in the workplace was possible, since My BFF's husband conquered this. He used to work for our company and left to work for himself. He often boasted how much he loves his job. That it doesn't even feel like work to him anymore. If that feeling exists for one person, then I will hold on to it and make it a goal for myself. I believe it is possible to achieve a work-filled happiness. I also believe if you want it, you have to go out and find it yourself.

It was the Friday before the weekend that My Boss would return. Since my story was somewhat solid, I started to write my first and only resignation letter. I obviously did not have any experience in quitting. I was only used to internships ending their course. But if I was going to quit, I wanted to be the best quitter in the game.

There are only two things I have ever quit in my life. Tennis, because I am simply not good, and gymnastics, because my brain didn't like to flip upside down. Understandable. So I found something I was actually good at and stuck to it. Dance. I loved it and I know that being a dancer shaped who am I today. I learned to hold myself accountable individually, but also in a group as a team. I have brought this knowledge with me through every phase in life, including my job.

Then, after fifteen years of competitions, I retired my dancing shoes. It took a toll on my social life and I wanted to enjoy my senior year of high school as a free to-be-teen. Dancing molded me mentally and physically, and it's the one activity I never stopped doing for fun.

My Office Neighbor, who worked in one of the offices with real cement walls next to mine, was my other BFF who helped me greatly with quitting. Since she has had more experience leaving jobs than I did, she helped me write my resignation letter after filtering through hundreds of Google templates for the perfect one.

"Is it awkward that I'm using their printer and envelope to give my resignation letter?" I ask.

"No, you're giving it back to them anyway," she replies.

That's true.

The weekend before I quit felt like the week before going on winter break in college. When I finished a fall semester in Orlando, I would take my last final and bolt out as fast as I could run. I had my car packed with every essential from my apartment so that I could haul ass straight home from the classroom. On my drive down, I would notice each leaf that was a tint of red and orange. Non-Floridians refer to these colors as "fall," and these leaves were the closest things I had to any type of season. I would open my sunroof and slightly crack the windows to breathe in the cool, fresh air. This is the feeling I looked forward to every December. This is the feeling I look forward to now. Freedom.

Monday, June 27th:

Desertion day. I wake up and nervous-poop three times before making the most crucial decision of the morning: picking out my quitting attire. If Nordstrom had a quitting collection in their catalogue, I wanted to resemble the *Chicest Quitter in The Game*. I decide on a dark blue jean, black satin long sleeve, and my black Tory Burch loafers because, if someone wears loafers, you have to take them seriously. I wear my hair slicked back in a ponytail, trying to be sophisticated and complex as possible. I was not going to look young today.

I arrive at work before anyone else, so I can internally rehearse my speech and practice non-fidgety movements. I slide an envelope underneath my keyboard while focusing on taking silent deep breaths, and concentrating on not throwing up.

I log onto Gchat to see if anyone else is online to quiet my overabundant thoughts. Yves is three hours behind in California, but sometimes she pulls an all nighter and I hope she is awake. I start to type a message when I hear footsteps coming closer from the front door. I gaze slightly over my shoulder to see who is pacing down the hall and it is who I least expect. My Boss! I am caught in a shocked, motionless stare when she wishes me a good morning. I flash an awkward, speechless grin, literally on the brink of shitting my pants.

Oh my God. This is real. This is real. My hands are shaking.

Brittany: "YVES WAKE THE FUCK UP I'M ABOUT TO QUIT MY JOB AND IM FREAKING OUT. WHERE ARE YOU?????"

8:51 AM:

I can sense the tumbleweeds passing by as My Boss and I sit alone in this office desert. Where is everyone? I need emotional back up! I push back my chair and quietly tip toe to the kitchen so she doesn't hear me. I decide to make myself a morning espresso, removing myself from the tension so we do not breathe the same morning air. It is so quiet in this office I feel like she can hear my heavy breathing. The moment I press brew, I hear her footsteps, and she emerges at my left. Doomed.

"Are you okay?" she asks.

"Yes," I say, recklessly collecting my creamer so I can dash as fast as humanly possible. Can this machine drip any slower!?

I'm beyond uncomfortable. I know I'm quitting… she does not. I am normally not this tense, but she is standing right over my shoulder watching the coffee drip into my cup. I feel like she thinks I'm giving her my espresso, but jokes on her. I'm def not.

The coffee spits its last drip and I sprint back to my desk. Frantically tapping my feet on the floor, I drum my finger against my computer mouse waiting, waiting, and waiting, until FINALLY My BFF signs on. I run to her office literally breaking out into sweats, which is another reason why we should always wear black.

"Just relax. Take a breather. You know why you want to quit. Just be polite and honest. Stand your ground. Do not let her take advantage of you because she will try her hardest to keep you here," she lectures.

"I came here to take a breather because I CANNOT BREATHE!" I pace back and forth in her office and plop myself into her chair to sit. "Ok. Ok," I inhale deep and I let it out deep, "Here goes nothing." I give her a high five and walk back to my desk shaking as I chug my iced espresso.

9:10 AM:

My company operates on Instant Messenger so I send her an IM:

"Good morning, please let me know when you have a free moment for me to come in," I ask.

She says sure and I inhale the deepest breath of my life. I slide the sealed envelope from under my keyboard and approach her office door. I knock twice and she waves me in. I turn to shut the door, trying to hide the envelope behind my thigh.

Before I can close it fully, she cries, "No. Please don't tell me that's what I think it is?"

HOW DID SHE KNOW? ALREADY?? Under boob sweat is in full stream.

I hold up my hand toward her, "Please don't make this any harder than it has to be." I gently move forward to the chair I regularly sit in when I come into her office. I set the envelope on the table placing one leg over the other and rest my body into the chair.

She pouts, "No, no, no. But why?"

I make sure to be consciously cautious in the tone of my voice as I answer. I wanted to transmit a calm, professional demeanor as I express my frame of mind. This may not be the last, but it was definitely the first time officially breaking up with a woman.

"In our conversation last week, I expressed to you all the challenges that both I, and our department face. Every time I try to provide solutions, you don't consider them. Trust me, I wish we didn't have problems here, but we do, and it can't be avoided any longer. I wanted to be in this managerial position so badly that I was willing to take on an overwhelming amount of work to gain the experience I so desperately yearned for. I did it, and I am so proud of myself. I am also extremely thankful for what you taught me and what I was able to do as a result. But the time has come where this is not for me anymore. I can no longer do three people's jobs; I simply do not have it in me. This position has created an emotional and mental imbalance that has affected my personality and this is not the person I want to be."

She glares and nods her head, "When I was traveling to meetings and I know it has been a few years, we were able to manage the responsibilities fluidly. I am not sure what has changed but you and your BFF should be able to be fine with the temps that we hire for you. I think your issue remains delegating responsibilities and if you were more effectual with that task, maybe we would not be sitting here discussing this," she says.

Although astonished, I remain calm and answer honestly, "I disagree. I delegate responsibilities just fine. When you hire temps, we don't know who we are getting. When I am provided temps at the age of sixty years old minimum, who can neither operate a computer, nor lift a forty pound box, who do not know which hand is left from right, I cannot do my job in the time allotted to set up an entire event. So it is not that I am unable to delegate responsibility, it is the fact that I am not given capable assistance for a job that six people collectively carried out when you used to travel. Now it is down to only two, who are rarely in the same room at one time."

"Well, we love you too much here to let you quit. I am not going to let that happen. I think you really need to think this decision through. You don't want to leave us. I know you. Look at how much you've grown in one year? I think you should take another twenty-four hours to make this decision," she debates.

"This is my final decision. You know, you told me from my first day if I was ever overwhelmed or felt I had too much on my plate, to let you know. And I let you know, didn't I?" I ask.

"Yes," she agrees.

"I never complained about the work I was doing. I never asked for any special treatment. All I ever wanted was to learn and to grow. I wanted more responsibility and education in this field. When I asked you to be a manager time and time again, and you finally, meritoriously gave me the opportunity. We came to one agreement: that I would take on a management position, but I would not be offered any help with any of my current duties in my existing position. I accepted knowing that if this workload had the capacity to drown me, I would be the only person who could save myself. I so eagerly wanted to learn, that I was willing to drown on my own. When I expressed that I needed help, you told me to put more hours in. And I did. But it was never the help I needed. I needed physical help for these meetings. The difference between my position and the one My BFF has is that she is a project manager. I was an assistant events coordinator. When I took on the project management position, I became both. Keep in mind, I took on my position when I started, and my predecessor's position when she left, plus the half she was doing for the doctors, and now a project management position. This was too much work for one person. Look how many people you didn't have to hire because I took on their roles?"

"Well, that is a part of the job. We all have to wear many hats in this company. Look what I do for all of the other departments. When someone slacks in their position, I take it up on my own to make sure it get's done or it falls on me," she claims.

"I totally agree with you, however, that is strictly your choice. People working here should not have the opportunity to slack in their jobs. How about when people say their own department needs help and you offer "Meetings" as a help aid. Guess what? Do you know who "Meetings" is? I am "Meetings." Me and only me. I cannot do my work, plus carry the work of our department, including every other department who have their own slothful assistants. I will not allow it…

Let me explain it this way. We have two people in our department: My BFF and myself. Her workload is one plate of food. My workload as a coordinator was my own plate of food. Since I became a project manager, I took half of My BFF's workload, hence, half of her plate of food. Now she has half a plate. I now have one plate and a half. Isn't that too much food for one person?" I ask.

Silence. I don't mess around when it comes to food. My last name is Berger for God's sake. I finally made her realize, yes, that is too much fucking food.

"Ok. I still won't let you quit. Take another twenty-four hours to think about this. Sleep on it and let me know what you think tomorrow. I just cannot accept this resignation letter today." She pushes the envelope in front of me, "I don't think you really want to do this." She rolls back to her computer monitor continuing to respond to emails, completely disregarding the rest of our conversation. The most important conversation of my life to date!

I thought I had just won my case. Why is she giving back my letter? Is this normal in quitting a job? I don't know. I had not prepared for this type of rebuttal, and, literally not knowing what else to do, I walk out of her office in defeat, with my envelope sealed in hand. I felt like I just made a huge mistake. I knew I wanted to quit; I don't need any more time. But she didn't accept my letter! Was that even allowed? I basically tried to quit and I failed. How could one fail at quitting?

I return to my desk and sit in my chair feeling my limbs go numb. My heart is still racing and I want to cry. This was the most difficult decision I was making in my life and now I feel eternally imprisoned by it. I take a deep breath and try to remember the reasons for quitting.

Every morning my alarm went off, my mind would cloud with depression in an already upset mood. If this happened every once in a while, it could be acceptable. But morning after morning, month after month, I endured the same melancholic imprint to get ready for another day of work.

My twenty-five-year-old goal to push myself out of my comfort zone was more than necessary. Comfortable. That was the place I always dwelled in. But the thing with comfort is that it doesn't help you grow. Comfort doesn't help you change or move on from challenging circumstances. I needed to feel uncomfortable for the first time, and this was just the begin-

ring a new version of myself.

ssage My BFF to tell her what happened and

My BFF: "ARE YOU FUCKING SERIOUS? THIS MAKES ME SO ANGRY! She is not allowed to do that! I told you she was going to try to play games with you and take advantage. Go back in there, give her your letter, and tell her you don't need any more time with your resignation. You made your decision and it is final."

My stomach is turning in knots and I feel like I'm going to be sick. But My BFF was right. The longer I sit here contemplating this decision, the longer I would be stuck here.

Through the reflection of my monitor, I see My Boss walk out of her office headed for the reception area. This is the time. I immediately race into her office, drop the envelope on her mouse, and speed walk back to my seat. I instant message her:

"Thank you for taking the time to speak with me this morning, but I took a lot of time to think about this decision and I do not want to delay my resignation any further."

My Boss returns to her office and sees my letter. She calls me back in and asks me to shut the door. I am not winning in a game where by default I am supposed to win. What is happening?!

"Brittany, I do not think you are thinking this through. Are you sure this is what you want to do because once I give this letter to the EVP-D and CEO, it is final," she contends.

"I know, but this is what I have decided," I answer.

I can sense her studying my face as if I am hiding some big secret and she finally asks, "Do you have another job lined up?"

"No," I reply.

"You can tell me if you do. We can have a bidding war on you," she jokes.

"No, I swear I don't. I haven't even looked," I answer.

"So why are you doing this? What are you going to do?" she asks.

I almost thought I was going to get away with not having to elaborate on my not yet finalized London tale. I didn't even factor in her bringing up a potential job hire as my reasoning for leaving.

"I was given an opportunity six months ago that I have accepted, to live in London for a couple of months while working for my friend's consulting company." Fiction for now, but I hope she believes it.

"What kind of consulting? Consultants fail most of the time in contracting for other businesses, you know," she kindly adds.

"Well, I'm not expecting to make this a full-time job with a high income. I am looking for a change in my current life and career. Some people never get a chance to move to another country and due to the following circumstances, I have decided I'm going to take it."

"I have an idea. What if I let you go to London for a month? You don't have to work. You can take a sabbatical for four weeks as long as you promise to come back. Would you be interested in doing that?" she asks.

Wow that is blindly generous. But I know how miserable I have been. Especially from being overwhelmed. Working isn't my sole purpose in life, as much as I have felt it has been. I refuse to be stuck again. I am leaving. "That is really kind of you to offer, but no. I'm sorry."

"But it gives you everything you want! You can get London out of your system, and then come back to work for us." She nods to herself, "Yes, I think you have been working so much, you have not had a vacation since last summer. I think you need this break. Then you will be fine and refreshed again."

I can't believe she is offering me this deal. But, I cannot go back on my word. I need to stick to my guns and get out of here. This is the chapter I need to close. No one said this would be easy, it definitely isn't... but I can see the light at the end of the tunnel and it is shining towards the Queen's palace. Sorry boss – no deal. "Thank you. I really do appreciate the offer, but my answer is still no," I conclude.

"How can I make you stay here? Your third year review is coming up next month. We were going to give you a nice raise, would $5,000 make a difference?" she asks.

Five thousand dollars, are you freaking kidding me? Of course that would not matter. For all of the work I have been doing saving salaries, healthcare, retirement for the multiple positions I have taken over, she should be giving me at least double that price. I am carrying this entire department and have never asked for more money than I have received, but I know now that I deserve much more.

"No, I'm sorry," I close.

"What if I just made you a project manager like you wanted and we'll figure out all of the other tasks later?" she asks.

"That isn't going to work because based on historical events, I know that, when that time comes, when I need the assistance, it will not be available to me. I am sorry if I am being too blunt, but we have been *down* this road before and I will not drive *down* that boulevard again. When my work pile overflows, I will still have to fulfill those time-consuming admin tasks. Don't get me wrong, I am not saying I am better than carrying out those tasks, I am definitely not. Everyone has to do them. There is just strictly not enough time in a day to get everything done one-handed. I am not asking to bow out of work I am already doing. I asked for assistance like everyone else does, I just never receive it, so this is the outcome," I reveal.

I am annoyed by the fact that she is slightly, finally giving me pieces of what I have politely, deservingly asked for, just because I am leaving. I already knew how important I was, as small, and as young as I may be. But now that she is realizing that time has run out and there is nothing else that can keep me here, she is creating a safety plan for herself.

"I'm sorry but plain and simple, there is nothing you can say or do to keep me here. I want to thank you for all of the opportunities over the past three years. I value every moment of the personal and professional growth it inspired. If only we were able to implement changes when I came to speak with you in the past, maybe we could have avoided this outcome. But this is my final change, and unfortunately it results in my leaving," I finalize.

"I understand," she says, "I will start the paperwork and communicate to the executives the news."

"Ok. Thank you," I finally, successfully brexit.

I leave her office confident in my decision, but also feeling like I was making the biggest mistake of my life. But that's only because she made me feel that way. I expected to feel more relieved than gloomed, but I was partially sad that this was the end of an era where I fought to remain for so long. I should have noticed the signs that this was not my final professional destination, and I recognize that now. I trust that the universe has greater plans for me, offering a plan I could not refuse in order to walk on the right path. A path where I am allowed to lead with my head and my heart. Where I would have the final say on what I will do with my future.

People, including my hairdresser frequently refer to me as sunshine. I enjoyed the label because of the involuntary brightness I could bring into a room. I missed what it felt like to radiate sunshine onto others, especially when I needed some shine for myself. This job made me feel like the light was far from my reach. I hit my lowest point when I returned home from work and saw my cheery mother at the door. She would ask one simple question and I would rudely snap at her for no reason at all. She never deserved any of it. She never deserved it and I couldn't control it. But working three jobs for months on end, I guess she expected some sort of outrage. One day, she finally snapped back asking, "What is the matter with yo ?"

And that is when I hit my rock bottom and confessed all of my unhappiness.

I never thought I would reach a point where I would wake up and fall asleep constantly fueled by anger. I was always able to overcome my negative emotions and transform it into progress. Not anymore. This was not me. I am a Leo! A fire sign, ruled by the Sun. I currently felt like tilapia, the bottom feeders of the ocean the Publix guy told me not to eat. But I chose to eat it anyway, continuing to feed my low self worth. Now, I know, I deserve the King Salmon or Kobe beef. This time, I choose to aim higher on the food pyramid because I deserve to eat like the Queen of the jungle.

Tuesday, June 28th:

Today marks the day I have less than two weeks left before cashing in my get out of jail free card. My brexit ball is in motion as my company goes through the measures to prepare for my official exit. The only part I look forward to is dressing up for my last days in the office. I have two weeks of coordinating my best professional looks of 2016, before transforming into a full-time uniformed Lulu Lemon mascot. Camp Equinox, it's been a while. I'm ready for re-enrollment.

I pull into the parking garage and back into the customary spot. Thirteen days until I won't have to do this anymore. I settle in at work making my routine espresso, parking my lunch bag in its standard space, and filling up my Blender bottle with water to stay hydrated for the day. I sit back into my chair and ponder when would be a good time to start packing up my belongings. I notice all the crap I have horded over the years on the perimeter of my desk. I throw out unnecessary objects one by one. It is still before 9:00 AM and I am alone on my side of the office enjoying the silence.

I decide to go through my emails looking for any communications that I may need to wrap up. I hear noises from afar as people start to arrive. From where I sit, I can see and hear everything. If we had a gossip column of what takes place on our floor, I would be the director of TMZ. I know what time people gradually decide to show up to work, the duration of their prolonged lingering morning coffee talks in the kitchen, the estimation of time their screen name idles when I know they are taking a paid, unnecessary long term shit in the office bathroom. I know it all and I can't wait to retire my TMZ hat.

My Boss walks into her office and closes the door behind her. Within two minutes, she requests my presence to quickly come inside. I put on my away message and pace to her office before she confirms with me one last time, "Are you positively sure you want to do this?"

"Yes," I answer.

"And you are only giving us two weeks, for sure?" she asks.

"Yes," I repeat.

"Ok. This is going to be very difficult for me to find a replacement in that short amount of time. Is it possible for you to give us one month so that you can properly train him or her in your duties?" she asks.

"I'm sorry, I can't. But I am happy to add all of my new responsibilities to the initial coordinator position I outlined for you."

"That's fine. Also, you will need to tell everyone in the company that you are quitting and what tasks you currently do for those departments. They will need to reclaim those responsibilities," she instructs.

"Ok, but you are also HR, shouldn't you be the one to tell them?" I ask.

"Normally, yes, but not in this situation. You need to tell them yourself," she orders.

Tell them myself? That is not my job. How unprofessional to have to tell them myself! If that is how you want to use my short time left here, that's fine. I'll awkwardly deliver the news. "Okay then."

She nods with a cold shoulder and turns back to her desk to open unread emails. I guess that was my cue. Easier for me to tell people I'm quitting than having to do actual computer work. So, I go one by one around the office to relay my own resignation news.

Some colleagues show excessive, sorrowful emotion, and some extreme enthusiasm for my next venture. I receive a mix of emotions but in all, my feelings are bittersweet. In this process, I put to rest a few key elements to my parting. In a business sense, I learned that I was a lot more resourceful than I originally thought. I validated that I was doing even more work for the company than I had noticed. There was not one division that I did not have a hand in. In a personal sense, I can't deny the strong relationships I have formed with my colleagues. One of my weaknesses I will never apologize for is for loving and feeling too much. I have gained beautiful relationships and wisdom from this work community who have become my other family. This is why I call it a divorce. It is not just work, it is personal.

Time is passing very slowly as I add the duties to my current position's document. Eighteen pages long, but who is counting. Today feels regularly uneventful on my end, but right before the clock strikes five, the shit literally hits the fan.

Background story:

One year ago, my company hired My Office Neighbor an assistant. This assistant became My Desk Buddy. Her role would be to survive the tasks that were previously dumped on me like everything else. I was assigned to be My Desk Buddy's mentor. This is the same girl I took out to lunch on her first day, to convince her that this job was the greatest role on earth. Yet, I was just putting on the greatest act on earth. Initially, I was thrilled to find that they were hiring a young employee who I would discover was only a month younger than I. At the beginning, I felt protective of her when I had to show her the reigns of the kingdom.

She was stationed in the cubicle behind mine. Since we didn't have cubicle walls, everything was out in the open. I have to admit, I was excited to have someone to share my annex with. I appointed her the co-host to my TMZ channel, sharing laughs, eye rolls, and loud sighs of frustration in the office. We also shared the same hindrances of working for a company where there was no room for growth. She wanted to be in marketing, a department we didn't have. And I just wanted to grow. An evolution that was not possible. I piqued her interest in astrology because we both felt torn in our careers and wanted third party guidance from the stars. We constantly referred to our horoscopes to help guide us towards our future unknown paths. "Trust the universe," my Spiritual Gangster shirt preaches. So, we did.

Half way through the year, her path veered into a different lane than she imagined but when the time came, she veered with it. From one assistant position to another, our CEO's Executive Assistant was going on maternity leave and needed a replacement. Since they have a hard time finding those, they recruited from in-house. My Desk Buddy was asked to take the CEO's Executive Assistant's place for three months, until she had returned. She asked for my advice and I told her to take it. She had nothing to lose. After the three-month mark, My Desk Buddy was to return to her prior position, but she had decided it was something that she no longer wanted. She had dreams of leaving the company and following her passion, which, of course, I always encouraged. "The only person getting in the way, and stopping you from getting what you want is yourself," I would advise.

My Desk Buddy no longer wanted to be an assistant and trust me, I get it. Like myself, she was not My Office Neighbor's assistant; she was the assistant to My Office Neighbor. She assisted with principal duties, not booking personal manicures and facials. Now that we have that clear, once the CEO's Executive Assistant came back from maternity leave, and all was supposed to go back to normal, My Desk Buddy decided she was no longer interested in her old position. She wanted to create her own role within the company until she would find a new job elsewhere. Unheard of? Totally, but I am always a cheerleader for other people's happiness, so of course I helped guide her towards her dream. Of course I helped her with her resume and email communications. That is what mentors do to mentee's, especially ones who become friends.

Why is this backstory important? Because this development occurred at the same time I put in my resignation. They say, "Everyone is replaceable," but I never believed that about myself. I did with other people, but not with me. Not because I'm overconfident in regards to my work ethic, but because I am confident in my work and in my job. No one cares about their jobs. They just want to collect their paychecks and get the hell out of there once the clock strikes 5:00 PM. People are replaceable for sure. I on the other hand knew I wasn't.

For weeks, My Desk Buddy was waiting to have a meeting to discuss future opportunities in-house with My Boss. She was waiting for the time when she would discover if it was her time to stay or to go. This afternoon, she tells me she is going in for the meeting. I remind her to stand her ground and fight for what she wants. I carry on with my work and realize two hours have passed. She has not returned to her desk. I look over my shoulder and also notice My Boss is absent from her office as well. This can't be good.

I call to My Office Neighbor and ask if she has seen My Desk Buddy, when she shakes her head in dismissal. Immediately, I think the worst, and predict she must be sobbing in the bathroom or in a closed office. I should be there for her, I thought, so I go looking for her. I finally find her leaning forward in a chair, in the Accounting Girl's office, with her arms crossed. I knock and walk in to see how she is doing.

"Hi! Are you okay? What happened?" I inquire.

She meets eyes with the Accounting Girl and they both look back at me.

"What?" I ask.

"Well, I don't know how to say this. She didn't really have any options for me and I don't want to go back to the position I was in before, so she offered me your position," My Desk Buddy reveals.

"My position? How? You have never planned a meeting before nor have any event experience," I laugh, "I thought you weren't interested in the meetings department, are you?" I ask.

The Accounting Girl answers for her, "I think this could be a really great opportunity for her. She could learn a whole lot and it would be something new, she may realize, she likes."

"I understand, but the one time My Boss gave My Desk Buddy an Excel project to do for our CEO, she had a panic attack because she was overwhelmed and I ended up finishing it for her. That is a pimple of the work I have to deal with from My Boss on a daily basis. She hates working for my boss," I explain, "Why would you do that to yourself?" I ask My Desk Buddy.

"I really don't know what to do right now and I don't want to go back to my desk," My Desk Buddy answers. "Well you don't have to. My Boss already left," I told her. "Honestly, the position she will offer you is going to be my lower administrative tasks when I first started here. It is like excessive homework but if that is what you want, take it. I can't see her having you be a project manager since I had to pull teeth for that, but that is also something I personally really wanted. I just want to let you know, you have it so easy with your boss now I wouldn't leave it. My Boss rules a world where the only outcome is to drown."

"I am not sure what I am going to do. I am going to think about it. But, I may take it. Will you be mad?" she asks.

"Of course not! I'm out of here. I just feel bad for you because you see first-hand what I go through daily. You are always mentioning how you don't know how I put up with her. But, I loved the work I was doing as a manager that I was willing to take all the shit I was given. Since you know how unhappy it made me, I feel bad that because I am leaving, my position is being thrown upon you. I wouldn't wish my job upon anyone, especially you," I answer.

I felt so torn with this situation. A part of me felt bad that, because I was leaving, she may have been given an ultimatum, to take Brittany's job or there won't be a job for you. Then again, I don't even know if that was the case at all. Second, there was definitely an untold story here that I can sense they are hiding from me... I can't put my finger on it. Third, this girl would definitely want to run and hide in my position. She absolutely hates My Boss and doesn't even work for her. Why is she even considering this? There is something I don't know here and I need to figure it out.

I run to My BFF and tell her what I just heard. With this information, she invites My Office Neighbor into the conversation. I report all of the details I gathered. My poor Office Neighbor feels subjectively hurt to hear that my position was offered to her assistant. She already created the list of duties to review with her in transition back into her assistant title. She was pissed that My Boss didn't have the courtesy to discuss this with her beforehand. The clock strikes end of day when My Desk Buddy taps on the office door.

"Hi guys," she says and leans against the wall. "I have something to tell you. I don't know how to say this, but I don't want to ruin anything between us, so I think you should know now," she shifts her attention to face me.

"Oh-kay?" I answer questionably.

"I wasn't offered your job when you started here... I was offered a higher full-time position of yours as a Senior Events Manager. She offered to hire me an assistant to help me with the other stuff you did, including an office and a salary increase," she exposes.

"Wait - WHAT? Are you sure?" I snapped.

"Yes," she answers looking down at her feet.

My chest clenches and I am unable to release a breath. In shock, I tightly grasp the bars of my chair and literally start to hyperventilate. This girl, who has no event background whatsoever, was offered my entire job on a silver platter just because I was leaving? ARE YOU FUCKING KIDDING ME? Benefits I had never asked for and were neither offered, nor attainable, were handed to her just because I wanted out? This is a huge slap in the face for everything I had worked for and forfeited.

"I don't understand. Did you tell her you were looking for other positions in the company that were marketing related?" My BFF asks.

"I was about to, but when I started telling her how I didn't want to go back to my old position," she stares at My Office Neighbor, "no offense, she said she had a brilliant idea of offering Brittany's job to me. I told her I didn't know if I was interested in it. That is when she offered me an assistant, an office, and a very large raise that I could really use," says My Desk Buddy.

My Office Neighbor responds, "This is fucking bull shit, sorry. Brittany this is a huge stab in the back to you. I am so sorry. This place is so fucked up. You don't deserve this," she faces My Desk Buddy, "Regarding you, I am so upset right now I can't even help you with a decision –"

"Your office line is ringing," My BFF says to My Office Neighbor.

"Oh shit, be right back," My Office Neighbor sprints out of the room leaving us behind.

I stare at the wall next to where My Desk Buddy is standing and try to gather my thoughts, "I don't know what to say. It makes sense now why you were being so quiet in the Accounting Girl's office. I just don't know how to feel because I worked so hard in this position, through every hoop of fire I had to jump through, to then be at a dead end and forced to jump off the cliff with no other options. You didn't have to do anything close to any of that. Everything I worked for and dreamt of is being given to you, unearned," I start to break down, "I am sorry for being frank but this is the most fucked up situation. I am not mad at you," I turn to My Desk Buddy, "you do what you want." I gaze back to My BFF, "I worked so hard for everything that was offered to her, to be shut down time and time again until I was drained and now I am drained dry," I look at the clock and wipe my tears, "I have to go." I leave sobbing as My BFF's tears were also at a peak of overflow. Both of us knowing that this was the definition of injustice in the workplace.

I walk back to my desk and close my computer, shoving it into my desk drawer. I forcefully take out my bag and run in the direction of the elevators. I don't want anyone to see me unraveling. I hold in my tears until I get to my car so I can emotionally explode. I worked so hard in this company. I thrived on the pride I generated, to then feel like it got shit on by my own Boss. The day after I quit! That was a strong turn around to cover your ass – I see that now. But it doesn't make it right or fair, and even though things in life aren't fair, I will make sure that fairness is achieved if it is the last thing that I do.

I turn on the ignition in my car and immediately call my mother. My emotions take over and I submit to another break down. I replay the sequence of events that occurred in the last moments of this afternoon as she tries to calm me down. The more I express, the more distress I feel. My mother asks to meet me at my favorite sushi restaurant, Fuji Hana, to continue the story there, instead of getting worked up while driving. I agree and meet her at the restaurant.

I pull in and take a look in my sun visor mirror noticing the red dots forming underneath my eyelids. I pat down the swollenness with my fingers, which does not help. I keep my sunglasses on, even though night has fallen and immerse myself into the booth. My mom gets up and gives me a big hug, which of course makes me cry even more. Luckily the ginger salad waiting upon my arrival stalls the tears from flowing long enough for me to continue the story. Fuji Hana has the best ginger dressing ever created, by the way. I still buy it in tubs. I finish playing back the office chronicles when she reinforces, "This is just another reason why you wanted to leave in the first place. You have a couple of days left and then you are absolutely done. Just think, it's better that you are quitting now rather than later, and if anyone knows how great you are, it's us, and most importantly yourself. As long as you know that, that is all that matters."

She was right. I needed to be reinforced that I was fucking great. No matter what they do, they could not replace me. But why should I care to be replaced when I was already the happiest character in *Les Mis*? A dark cloud would follow my predecessor after my sunshine has been removed. I folded my legs in Indian style and brought both hands to my heart's center, "Namaste," I exhale. "All will be well with the world. Maybe I shouldn't go back tomorrow, what do you think?" I ask.

"Ask your father. If it were up to me I would drive there myself, pack up your shit and flick everyone off in my trail."

I laugh. I now see where I get my humor. My spicy, crunchy tuna roll arrives when my phone starts to ring and flashes, My BFF.

"Hello?" I answer.

"You are not going to believe what just happened. Hold on, I'm getting on the train," she rushes.

"Uh-oh. Should I stop eating? Nah I'm not going to stop eating, but let me know when you're ready. What more could have happened after I left?" I answer in full nosh.

"So, your Office Neighbor was so hurt by what happened and how your Desk Buddy refused to work with her anymore, that your Office Neighbor went into another employee's office to vent and started bawling in distress."

"No way, is she okay?" I ask.

"Well, after you left we all gathered in that office to talk about what had happened. They couldn't believe it and really felt for you. Then, your Office Neighbor was so upset, thinking how could she possibly be a bad boss with everything she has done for your Desk Buddy..." she continues.

"Right, she even bought her a Marc Jacobs crossbody. That's a really great boss to me," I convince.

"Haha right! Well, your Desk Buddy told me in private, that she didn't want to do "bitch work" for your Office Neighbor anymore. So I obviously told her because she is my friend more than your Desk Buddy is. That's what made her so upset," she reveals.

"HOLDDD ONNN A SECOND. Bitch work? She doesn't even know what bitch work is if it hit her in the face! I am Queen bitch of bitch work. Everyone's gotta pay their dues. I can't believe she said that," I say.

"Yes!" My BFF shouts, "So your Desk Buddy sees us gathered in the office and walks in. Your Office Neighbor confronts her asking *why did she spread that she was doing bitch work for her, to the point where she no longer wanted to work under her anymore? Why didn't she talk to her about it?* It sparked into this whole thing and everyone just started arguing and crying..."

"Holy shit. No way!"

"Yes way! So now, I am finally on my way home after cleaning up this mess and tomorrow should be a very interesting day in the office. And I need a drink!" she announces.

"Oh my god. I literally cannot believe this is happening. I should drink too but I'm eating my calories instead of drinking them," I declare.

"What are you doing?" she asks.

"I am enjoying a delicious sushi roll with my mother. I cannot believe all of this happened! This is crazy. Ok, I have an idea. Tomorrow, shit is going down, and we will not enter the war without a fight. Send out a raven and text the team to wear black because tomorrow starts Day 1 of Game of Thrones," I command.

I am Khaleesi and winter is coming. Let the games begin.

The Silver Platter

Wednesday, June 29th:

I stand in front of the mirror with my hair parted and slicked back in a low pony. I dress in uniform of head to toe black with a thick gold necklace resting on my collarbone. I fasten my booties so my heavy footsteps will echo down the hallway. (The hallway is carpeted, but I'll step with all my might to make sure that shit echoes). I take a seat in my cubicle throne until the hour of nine flashes on my screen.

Even though I look like a badass motherfucker, I am slightly shaking inside. My team rolls in deep, wearing black as instructed, resembling a nightmare worse than the death eaters in *Harry Potter and the Prisoner of Azkaban*. My Boss walks in late and bids her morning greeting. I purposely ignore her because I am unapologetically pissed off. I can't even bring myself to meet her eyes in passing. *HOPE YOU SLEPT WELL LAST NIGHT, BECAUSE YOU GON' LEARN TODAY! (Kevin Hart voice).* The well-raised side of me prides myself on being a professional. Even in my darkest, moodiest moments I still attempt to keep my cool. But today is not that day. Today, I only see one color, and that color is red.

She walks past my desk to make her coffee and then circles back around to ask me a question. My eyes do not leave my computer monitor. She asks me if I'm okay and I respond dismally, "I'm fine."

She heads into her office and I hear My Office Neighbor follow behind, "Fuck it. I'm going in," she says.

"You go girl." I whisper. "Leave the door cracked open," I add.

"Shut up," she responds and slams the door closed.

I kick off the wall and roll my chair to the farthest point of my desk, attempting to do my best listening. I lean to the right trying to open my ears as radio signals. But before I can prepare for Act I of my Yenta debut, I hear a loud bang on her desk and anxiously speed walk to My BFF's office. My territory was no longer a safe zone.

Not even two minutes pass and My Office Neighbor appears at the door. She knocks on the glass and scares the shit out of us.

"WHAT HAPPENED?" I ask.

"I'm freaking out. She just quit," she paces.

"WHAT! What do you mean quit?" I shout.

"I swear. She just quit. I'm freaking out. I walked in there and said we need to have a very serious conversation. I don't appreciate you offering my employee a position change when it wasn't even discussed with me, her supervisor. I think this is extremely unprofessional and poorly mismanaged, especially with all that was done to Brittany."

My Boss looks up, "What do you mean what was done to Brittany?"

"How you offered my assistant Brittany's glorified position because she decided to quit. This is very premature and a total stab in her back, in my opinion," My Office Neighbor explains.

"Hold on. How do you know about this?" My Boss asks.

"Because Brittany told me," My Office Neighbor replies.

"How does Brittany know?" My Boss asks frantically.

"BECAUSE MY ASSISTANT TOLD HER EVERYTHING!" My Office Neighbor shouts.

My Boss widens her stare with tears of shock welling her eyes. She yells under her breath, "This is bullshit. I am done with this. I quit." She packs her things in tears repeating, "I knew this was going to happen. I knew it! Why do they always make me the bad guy? I'm done." Then she left the office.

My BFF looks at me, "I can't believe this. This is insane."

"Ohhh my goddd!" I buzz, "I told you guys the shit would hit the fan when I left, but I didn't know how massive the shit would be!"

"Does that mean you're going to stay now if she never comes back?" My BFF asks.

"Hell no! I say let's leave now. Ugh, I didn't even get a chance to release the dragons in my outfit," I slick my hair back and tighten my pony, "I'm sad."

"Cheer up Khaleesi, we need to figure this out. She can't just quit. We need to tell the EVP-D when she gets here. I'm still pissed off by all of this. This is so unethical," My Office Neighbor says.

I feel like I'm living in a real-life movie scene. I cannot believe all of this is going down. I sprint down the front hallway, cut right, and sprint all the way down the main hallway until I reach my other employee-mates to broadcast the news. I CAN'T BELIEVE THIS! This is when I knew that reasons for my fight were 100% accurate. The EVP-D (D - daughter of the CEO) walks in chirpy and My Office Neighbor bolts through her door before she can set down her belongings.

"Hi. Sorry to burst in here but did you hear?" she asks.

"Hear what?" EVP-D asks.

"That The Boss quit?" My Office Neighbor reveals.

"What are you talking about?" the EVP-D replies.

"Oh my god. Ok. Um… do you have a couple of minutes, or maybe an hour?" My Office Neighbor looks at me and shuts the door.

I do what I do best and run into the office next door, placing my ear against the wall to try to listen to their conversation. Their words are mumbled and I can't decipher them into sentences. Fail. I sit back at my desk and try to listen from my post, hearing faint remarks. "She'll come back. She has to. She has been here for ten years. This is all blown out of proportion... Yes, I agree we should have spoken to you first..." Yada, yada. My Office Neighbor walks out from the office back into hers. I instant message her.

Brittany: "HELLO?? WHAT DID SHE SAY?"

My Office Neighbor: "Not now."

Brittany: "YES NOW. Tell me. Quickly, or I'm coming in there."

My Office Neighbor: "Fine. I told her what happened. She didn't make it a big deal. She said everything would be worked out and I told her she needed to talk to you. She didn't think she did until I told her you were aware of everything."

Brittany: "Uh-oh. Okay. Thanks for the update."

My Office Neighbor: "You're welcome you little squirt."

I put on my away message and walk to My BFF's office. She's on a call and waves me in to quietly enter. I sit in the chair across from hers observing her somber expressions until she hangs up the phone. "What now?" I ask.

"That was her," she replies.

"WHAT DID SHE SAY?" I ask.

"I feel bad for her," she says.

"Of course you do, because you have a heart. I did too once, but she turned it into coal. What did she say?" I ask.

"She confirmed that she sent an email resignation to the CEO and EVP-D, that she is leaving the company due to the circumstances that came about with your resignation. She was hysterically crying on the phone. I have never heard her voice screech that way. It was heart-wrenching… it was," she exhales.

"Okay… and?" I ask.

"You know she never curses, and she said numerous times, word for word, *'this is so fucked up.'* She feels horrible about what was done to you. She said that none of this is right and she should have pushed back and fought for you with the CEO and EVP-D. She realizes now that she didn't fight enough for what you wanted and you were *her* employee. That you did deserve all that you worked for and that she knows you asked her for help. She knows you wanted to grow, but when she spoke to the CEO and EVP-D about it they said you didn't need to grow right now. She repeated to me how unfair this was to you and she would never want to make you upset. She admitted that she failed you as a manager and how she saw you as the daughter she never had. She feels horrible and responsible that this happened to you," she finishes.

"Well… that's good in the sense that at least she can admit what she did was wrong. Ugh now that you tell me this like, thanks, but this happened to *me* - I'm sorry! No one else here is allowed to play the victim. I'm not even playing the victim and I *am* one. I am the one who is quitting because of all of this shit, and now everyone else wants to play the "poor me" card because they got called out? No thanks! I'm not buying it, not even at a discount. I am the one who should be apologized to. I am the one who should be explained exactly what was done and why, and right now in this moment I am not sorry that people are crying and feeling bad for themselves. No one took into consideration how this would affect me, while I'm still working here for the next two weeks. Could have waited a little more than half a second, instead of moving forward the very, next day!"

I shoot up from her desk and walk back to mine, infuriated. I wiggle my mouse so my monitor wakes from sleep mode. My Office Neighbor steps out of her office and pauses. I look up.

"What?" I ask.

She points assertively to her right and starts to head for the kitchen. I look around and count to ten until following behind. We meet in the back blind spot of the galley.

"I have something to tell you, but you are going to freak out… so don't freak out," she insists.

"Okay…" I say.

"Promise me you won't freak out," she urges.

"I promise!" I raise my palms in reassurance.

"When I spoke to the EVP-D, she didn't understand why you would care that your position would be offered to your Desk Buddy. Your Boss described your reasoning of leaving as 'going to London to gallivant around and live out a life's dream.' She painted a picture that working no longer suits you and you don't have to work anymore since you still live at home. This is why she didn't feel she needed to speak with you. When I told her that reasoning was completely false, I insisted she speak with you to get your side of the story."

"Are you fucking kidding me?" I retort.

"Shh… I told you not to freak out! Don't make it obvious. Go back to your desk and try to relax because she will probably call you in any minute," she exits the kitchen and I pull out the chair behind me to sit.

This woman made it seem like I was leaving this company to go have fun in London?! I don't think so. I hesitantly proceed to my desk and am welcomed with an instant message from the EVP-D.

EVP-D: "Hi, can you come in?"

Brittany: "Sure."

I chug half of my water bottle, take a deep breath, and make my way to her office. I knock and she smiles as I sit in the chair directly across from her. Normally I could fake a smile, but now my face is expressionless. I feel my voice shake when I attempt to speak so instead I allow her to speak first.

"How's it going?" she asks upbeat.

"Well, we both know how it's going," I answer, shifting uncomfortably in the chair.

"Yes, it's seems to have been an eventful morning. I know some rumors have been thrown around the office so I wanted to see if there was anything you felt the need to ask?" she inquires.

Rumors? That's another joke I'll add to the books. I very much respected this woman. I really liked her as well. Some in the office did not. Maybe because she was their boss and they were intimidated by the fact that she possessed a higher title than them, aside from also being the CEO's daughter. None of that mattered to me. With a significant difference in the hierarchy ladder of her position compared to mine, I really enjoyed her company as a person. Maybe because she was also Jewish and I felt we shared a natural, unspoken bond? But at this point, all bonds were clearly broken and I had enough of the bullshit already. Too much shit had already hit the fan. It's time to clean it up in the only way I know how, with honesty.

"I'm not sure when my exit interview will be, but I think it's best that we just get it over with now," I look up to meet her eyes and she looks surprised. She leans back into her chair and crosses her arms.

"Ok," she agrees.

Here comes the waterworks of sweat. I remind myself to speak slowly, "You know, I replayed two outcomes in my head as to how I wanted this conversation to go for my exit interview. The first was entering your office and having a pleasant and professional conversation... thanking you for the opportunity to work here and leaving this job in a contented manner.

The second was to maybe reveal to you all of the challenges my department has faced over the years I've been here, generally because I didn't want to only talk about myself leaving, even though we are having this conversation because of the fact that I am indeed, leaving. But, I also wanted to present to you solutions moving forward on how this department could reach its highest potential. Both scenarios were amicable.

Now, with everything that has happened over the past couple of days… I think I'm going to throw both options out the window. I've never been good at sugar coating things, so I'll be frank. Let's start from the beginning and, mind you, this may take a while. I've never been very good at telling short stories," I adjust.

"When I first started here, I was a sponge. Able to absorb all information and soak everything in. This is what I think is so great about hiring young, fresh, employees out of college because they don't have prior experience that already molded them into a specific position. They are untouched. You can mold them yourself into anything you want them to be. I wasn't given significant responsibilities at the beginning because my position was being formed day by day. But my mentor left and I took on her job, including the half she was already doing from her neighbor, and my full job… I was given a lot more to do. And that was okay with me.

With all of this, I still wanted more. I asked for more responsibility and more work because I wanted to learn as much as I could, but My Boss put a halt to that for one sole reason. I was too young. I asked not once, but four times to be a manager. Not for a raise or an office, just for the experience to grow because I so desperately wanted to do more. I fought and fought just to learn and that shouldn't be looked down upon in any company.

When I was finally given the opportunity to be a project manager, I knew I had a lot to prove. I wanted this position so badly I was willing to have an overwhelming, sleepless year to gain that experience. I knew that I had more eyes watching me than anyone else because honestly, My Boss was probably waiting for me to fail. And you want to know why I didn't? Because I knew that the second I messed up, whether it was my fault or not, all of this would be taken away from me, and I would never get this opportunity again. I had so much more to lose than any other member of this company, so I made sure everything was beyond perfection. I had a back up, to the back up, to the back up, to a point where due to my success, My Boss asked me to take over future meetings no one else had time to handle. Now why did no one else have time? Because we are severely understaffed. It may not look that way, but it's true because I myself was doing four people's jobs and I have finally had enough of the oversight.

What I am hurt by the most on the coat tails of my leaving is everything that happened yesterday. My Boss came to you and relayed that I was moving to London because I wanted to carry out a "life's dream"? That is absolutely not the case. I am quitting because I would rather be unemployed than continue to work under her management. I never thought I would admit that to you, but that is the honest truth. I worked so hard to earn this position. I never asked for a thing I did not deserve.

To hear that my glorified job was handed to a girl on a silver platter, with no experience, not one inch of desire for working in this field is insulting.

I went through an emotional roller coaster of ups and downs and at my lowest point, I decided to leave because being unhappy had become my natural state. I hated who I became working under her. And just to make it clear, My Boss confirmed there was no other option for me to stay here, so I felt pushed out. It felt more of a force than a choice. And I was not offered one thing to stay. Even if she did, it wouldn't have changed my mind. But the fact that she never offered me anything close to what was offered My Desk Buddy is just impolite. She never had to offer me anything but growth because that was the only thing I was after.

The one entity I value most from this entire working experience is my pride. How proud I am of myself for everything I was capable of doing and how I grew as a person. How much I accomplished on my own that was earned, not given to. No one here can take that away from me and for that…" I pat myself on the back, "I am okay with leaving the way things are," I finish.

I feel my scar start to heal because I had said my peace and my reputation was no longer soiled. Nothing she could say would make a difference anyway. I was done.

"I am sorry that this is how you have to go out. I wish we could find a way for you to leave on a lighter note. We do love you in this company and wish you weren't going, but based on what you said, I sense that there's nothing we can say or do to keep you here any longer. It is a tough world out there and I hope that you are able to find what you are looking for in London. If you did ever want to come back here, there will always be a place for you and we will create one if need be. I can say for the CEO and myself that this is a loss and you were a great employee to have on our team.

Concerning your occupational growth, your Boss did inform us that you wanted to grow and take on larger responsibilities, but yes, you are young, so we didn't see the rush. Maybe that was our mistake and not realizing, not permitting that to you would cause you to leave. Regarding your position here, the way business works is when one position opens, we need to find someone to fill it. Since your Desk Buddy no longer wanted her position and honestly, we had nowhere to place her, we offered her your role. Since the CEO developed a strong bond with her while she filled in for his Executive Assistant, he wanted to make her an offer she couldn't refuse. I'm not sure exactly what she told you she was offered, but I am sure it was a miscommunication," she explains.

"No, it wasn't. She very clearly told me she was offered a Senior Events Manager position, with an office, an assistant, and a $10,000 pay increase. My family are private investigators so I collected all of my facts," I reply.

"And how do you know this?" she asks.

"Because she told me," I confirm.

"Well, she shouldn't have. That was supposed to be confidential information but, okay," she shakes her head, "Again,

Brittany, I am deeply sorry this all happened this way and I hope we can reach some type of neutral ground for your resignation."

"We can. I'm mentally drained, honestly. I'm not even miffed anymore now that I told you my whole biography, which, by the way, I appreciate you listening to. I just want to leave here on a high, positive note, if possible, and move on with my life," I resolve.

"Good to hear. Okay, well, I have some damage to repair so, let me get to it."

"Okay, thank you for your time," I say.

"You too, Brittany."

I walk back to my desk and take out a Kind bar. All of this honesty is making me hungry. Right when I think I can rest my voice, and my head, my Desk Buddy appears out of nowhere. She props herself on the wall of my cubicle as I tear open the wrapper.

"Hi," she salutes.

"Hi," I take a bite.

"Can we talk?" she asks.

"Now?" I continue crunching.

"Yes, or whenever. I feel like there is a lot of gossip around the office about me and since maybe I have made some new enemies, I wanted to make sure you weren't one of them," she says strictly.

"I'm not," I answer.

"So, where is your Boss and why were you running up and down the hallway earlier," she argues, "and why did you speak with the EVP-D for an hour?" she asks.

"Listen, I'm not able to discuss this with you, but since you feel out of the loop, My Boss just quit this morning because of all of this," I express.

"She what?!" she asks.

"She quit. Give me five minutes and we can go talk in a back office," I suggest.

"Wow. That's crazy! What happened?" she asks.

"Shh, I'll tell you in a few minutes. Go sit down," I demand.

"I have to go to the bathroom. When I come back, will you be ready?" she asks.

"Sure," I say trying to finish my bar.

It's amazing how no one lets me eat in peace around here. I check my empty inbox and she's back. It feels like the day is already over but sadly it's only noon.

"Ready?" she asks.

I nod.

We walk to a vacant back office used for storage and sit on the floor so no one can see us.

"Be honest… are you mad at me?" she asks.

"I'm not mad at you," I lie.

"You're lying," she says.

I knew I was lying. I didn't want to be mad at her but I naturally was! It's like the moment we try a new food and are instantly aware what we find delicious and what we don't. For me, this is how I feel about blue cheese. I naturally cannot stand blue cheese. When you experience that bad taste in your mouth, you automatically consider anything with that flavor distasteful. Cobb salads have blue cheese and therefore I don't like Cobb salads. But the Cobb salad has never wronged me. Just the blue cheese. Therefore, I can have a Cobb salad as long as I order it without. This is how I viewed this situation. My Desk Buddy is the Cobb salad. The Cobb salad is my friend. The blue cheese is not. Therefore, I should really be mad at My Boss, the blue cheese.

I look up at her. She looks sad. She was put in a situation she neither thought she would be in, nor ever wanted. Now, the one person she counted on was her opponent in who she could no longer confide. I would be out of here in a few days time, so in this instance, I choose not to share how I really feel about being the core of the chaos, or really about being the after thought. I choose to care less about how I feel deceived, and choose to forgive and let go.

"Ok I'll be honest…at first, I was angry and blind-sided by all that had transpired. I was upset with how you paraded the news to everyone in the office. I shouldn't be mad at you because you are the one who honestly revealed the situation to me. In the beginning, I did feel a little betrayed. But none of this is your fault. I am not mad at you. I am mad at My Boss. I am mad that I gave her my life and she turned it into dust. I will be here for you, and you have a brighter future, much brighter than the darkness that shadows this place. Looking at you, and knowing the misery I withheld for years in my position, I know it is going to be worse for you," I grab her hands, "I don't want that for you. If you think accepting this offer this will make you happier than you are now, then take it, but thinking about this just gives me a pit in my stomach," I express.

"Well, I wanted to tell you that I am not taking your job. When she first offered it to me, all I could think was thank you - but no thank you. Then when she offered me the office, the assistant, and the huge raise I thought, how could I turn this down?" she says.

"I know," I agree.

"But I am still waiting on Royal Caribbean to get back to me and I just want that to come through. Look what she did to us. She separated us. She tried to put this between us to ruin our friendship because she does not believe in work friendships. Why would I want to work for a woman like that? None of this is fair to you or to me," she fights.

She had a point. My Boss used to say to my colleagues, *"these aren't your friends, they are your coworkers. Remember the difference."* I strongly disagreed. We spend more time with our coworkers than our friends, traveling included. My Desk Buddy made our work annex more enjoyable to be in. We shouldn't be punished for it.

"You need to keep your eyes on the prize. Come," we walk over to our window filled conference room and open the shade. I point to the Royal Caribbean office across the bay over the bridge, "See the office right there? That is your future headquarters. Imagine yourself driving to work each morning, listening to your favorite song in the car, driving over that bridge, down the road into that parking lot. Envision yourself walking through those doors every morning, up the stairs or the elevator and walking to your desk. Putting your purse down, turning your computer on and getting a cup of coffee. If you envision that everyday, you will manifest what you want. The job will be yours."

She pulls me in for a big embrace. "Thank you! I needed that. I missed you," she says.

"Thanks. I am always here for you. Sorry I was distant. When I wear emotions on my sleeve they're also stuck on my face and nothing in this world can change that in that moment," I laugh.

"Now tell me what happened with your Boss."

I vaguely tell her the story. She asks about my conversation with the EVP-D and I don't disclose any details. Her mouth may be a loose cannon, but mine would be tight-lipped, only to release when intended.

Once I leave the office and settle into my car, I call my mother. First, she tells me about the latest Equinox gossip and how much money she saved at Bed Bath and Beyond using her coupons. I then give an hour long loaded recap of how the kingdom fell and rose to succession in one single morning. I was exhausted. But for the first time ever I did not want to hear myself talk any longer.

"Are you heading to the gym?" she asks.

"I really don't feel like it, but that still doesn't seem like a good enough reason not to go… I'm just not in a burpee kind of mood today, you know?"

"No one ever wakes up wanting to do burpees," she mentions, "Let me check my EQ app and see what other classes you can take. Oh! You should take yoga! You could use a guided internal reflection, or two," she laughs.

"You know what, that's a great idea. I just might," I decide.

My first and last yoga experience still remains back in Israel. Is yoga being called to me as an escape from mental strife? First, with Mr. GQ where I did anything but concentrate. Now, my focus shifts on the aftereffects of my job. Both subjects equally overpowered my mindset. This time, I am ready to unplug. I decide to give yoga a second chance. I need a rejuvenating 'Namaste' moment to get me through the rest of this week. It was only Wednesday, and at this rate, God save the Queen.

I lie on that mat and the lights start to dim. I close my eyes and try to think about the impossible "nothingness" of an empty mind. The music faintly sounds in the background and the yoga chimes begin.

"Yin yoga encourages concentration and focus of the breath. It is the practice of slowing the mind and accepting the release. Welcome," the instructor announces. Yin yoga restores the body by emphasizing long, slow, deep holds for 2-3 minutes. In Brittany terms, it is basically just a stretching class for normal humans who are not yogis. The tone of her voice has already calmed me and for once, I am completely focused on listening to her guidance instead of the chaos in my mind.

First step: Focus on the breath.

Breathing in deep inhales and breathing out deep exhales, I try to concentrate on the rise and fall of my belly. I remain focused for maybe six seconds. I obviously counted, until my mind wandered into any and every thought besides yoga. How much time has passed? What am I going to eat for dinner? Is my circulation going to be cut off in this position? Will my leg need to be removed? Sigh. This reminds me why I don't attend yoga.

Step two: Slow your mind.

Let's face it, impossible task.

Step three: Release.

Release, I can do this. Next pose. I align my legs straight in front of me, allowing my fingertips to reach near the floor, passing the bridge of my feet. I breathe slowly, and release. The instructor appears behind me, pushing my back forward and whispers, "let it go."

I close my eyes and reach further, remembering the vital importance of breathing, and how, if I stop, I may pass out. "Inhale," I take another deep breath in. With each breath, I notice I reach deeper into the stretch. Three minutes pass and I open my eyes. I realize by surrendering to the pain and following through with the breath, my nose reaches my knees and with constant focus, I am able to overcome the stretch.

I spend so much time thinking too much and assessing too much. After reminding myself to breathe, release, and let go, I am finally able to relax. On the rare occasion that I did attend yoga, I would practice just for the benefit of the stretch. Not for the benefit of the mind. I would only attend for what I felt I needed, not recognizing that I need both.

At what point do we gather that we need both and not just one? Regrettably, we grasp it when it's too late or when we need it the most. Would this practice of the mind have helped me in the past, before quitting? Probably not. But that is because quitting was inevitable. The end result was out of my control. I walked into this session creating an intention on what I wanted to accomplish today. Unbeknownst to myself, I did not anticipate the result of accomplishing what my soul needed. Both.

Thursday, June 28th:

Break-Fast

Thanks to yoga I went to sleep relaxed and wake up refreshed. This feeling reminds me of the morning back in Israel when I stepped out early and felt the urge to run. I loved that sense of drive; I want to grasp that same feeling at home. I switched up my morning humdrum and set my alarm an hour earlier to give myself unrushed time. I am so used to rushing from the moment my alarm sounds that I don't know mornings without a sense of urgency. My true test was to examine if I can adapt here, like I did in the desert.

My feet touch the floor and I stand not knowing what to do first. My routine was to walk straight to the bathroom, brush my teeth, start my face regimen, and, in between each step, make my bed, get dressed, and prepare my gym bag for the evening. This entire period takes approximately fifteen minutes. Then I make my breakfast, coffee, and lunch at the same time, to then eat in my car because time is always of the essence.

In the past three years, I have never eaten breakfast sitting at the table. Today, I decide to break the routine and break the fast to eat, not fast. Instead of entering the bathroom, I walk out my door to the kitchen and power on the Keurig. First, I brew my hot water with lemon. I proceed to the glass dining room table and choose the seat furthest away from the sliding glass door. I stare out at the ocean's darkest sea of blue and take my first sip of the day. Relaxing. Is this what retirement feels like? No wonder people love it. I feel myself wanting to look over at the clock but I force myself not to let time dictate my pace.

The apartment is so quiet I can hear my flesh leaving the stoned floor with every step. I find peace in the stillness. Watching the waves splash back and forth across the sand is serene. I now make a cup of coffee and can't identify whether I was sipping it slowly because I was enjoying it, or because it was burning hot. I have so much time to enjoy this morning that it's starting to feel like a weekend. Maybe this is the solution to the bad news bears of the morning rush.

This cause and effect of rushing makes us prone to having a potential bad day. One thing doesn't go our way and we blame waking up on the wrong side of the bed. We blame the coffee for spilling on our shirts, we blame the traffic for being late for work, and we blame whoever was home at the time when we left our phones on the counter. We blame everything we can, when the real fault is on us. I am a victim of loving my sleep. I would rather sleep twenty more minutes a night than wake up twenty minutes earlier to avoid rushing. I used to think rushing was destined, until today.

I hear the elevator sound and the front door swings open where my dad appears coming home from the gym. He squints to test his vision to confirm that I am, indeed, sitting at the table at 6:00 AM. I can hear the rock music blasting from his headphones as he pauses his iPod to remove his ear buds.

"I'm sorry, am I seeing this correctly? Are you sleep walking or are you really up this early?" he asks.

"I am trying an experiment," I answer.

"An experiment? Ok. An experiment of being an early riser or what?" he places his backpack on the floor and leans up against the bar.

"I'm trying to see if I'm capable of enjoying a morning without rushing. Starting with drinking coffee and eating breakfast, in a seat," I confess.

"What a concept," he adds.

"Right? Want to try it?" I ask.

"No, I have things to do," he answers as he walks into the kitchen.

"Well, so do I, and you work for yourself so technically you can make your own hours… I still have to make breakfast. Do you want me to make you something and you can sit with me?" I ask.

"I don't eat breakfast," he responds.

"You're impossible. You should because breakfast is delicious and the most important meal of the day. What if I eat and make you coffee and you can sit with me?" I propose.

"Fine. Give me five minutes to shower," he answers.

"Fine," I excite.

I grab my breakfast ingredients and slow myself down to make my food. Intentionally moving slowly is the weirdest feeling as a fast pacer. I am happy to be succeeding in my first attempt of this new nature. I catch myself wanting to look at the clock every five seconds but try my hardest not to. My dad comes out of his room and joins me at the table. He isn't much of a talker most of the time, so we sit gazing out at the water and the clear morning sky.

"Nice view," he comments.

"I know, right?" I agree. "I was contemplating sitting outside but it's hot as balls and I don't want to sweat."

"Yeah you would melt out there," My dad has ADHD so I can tell he is getting anxious. "So, one week and one day left, how are you feeling?"

I take a bite of my delicious blueberry, cinnamon, agave mixed oatmeal before answering, "I feel… liberated… and scared… in control, but not in control. Self encouraged and externally discouraged. Is that how you're supposed to feel?" I ask.

"I don't know. You seem a little bit of everything. Which do you side with the most?" he asks folding his arms above his belly. I know what side I am feeling the most but not enough to say it out loud. I look for a blueberry and scoop it up, "I'm scared," I nod.

He tilts his head, "Scared of what?"

"That I made the wrong decision," I look down.

"Do you feel like you made the wrong decision?" He asks.

I tap on the back of my hard-boiled egg a few times until it cracks. Slowly picking apart the shell I deliberate my response, "I feel like the effect of everyone else's opinion is making me feel like I am making the biggest mistake of my life. But in my gut, I know I made the right decision. Six months ago, I knew I wanted to quit and I was sticking by that because every morning I woke up, I firmly wanted out. But every day I was anxious and that feeling never vanished. I tried to assure myself that I shouldn't be scared and sometimes it worked and sometimes it didn't. But after the shit storm that passed through this week, I am CONVINCED I did the right thing. It also doesn't help that my coworkers are making me feel like I am abandoning them, but they have their own opportunities to jump off the ship. I just jumped first."

"Maybe you will lead the pack and they will follow," he suggests.

"I don't think so. They have more to lose than I do. They have families to provide for and mortgages. Their life is kind of stagnant, but if they made themselves a goal to at least look for new ventures on the sideline, then they can enroll in a new race. But that's up to them. They are just comfortable, so sadly I don't think they'll ever leave."

He nods back, "Well, fortunately for you, you have nothing to be scared of… you saved a lot of money and you have us as a home base. Plus, you're a smart girl. I don't think you will make any stupid decisions. I do think it would be smart if you look for jobs now and maybe apply before deciding to go to London. What if you get a job you've always wanted? And if you don't get the job, then you can decide to go wherever and do whatever you want to do?"

"No. I am going to London," I strongly announce, "I looked for jobs and I am not interested in any of them. I didn't work my ass off juggling three jobs for no reason. This is my time to do what I want. I have had too many people make it seem like it is unwarranted that I have to go to another country to find "whatever I'm looking for." Fuck them. I am going because I want to attract an idea so much larger than anything I could ever imagine. I want to be in a new environment where there is no other option but to push myself beyond my limits. To prove to myself, *I can do this*. I will find my next venture. I am sure of that. But that is something I cannot do here," I finish my breakfast and take his mug from under his hand.

"Well if that's how you see it," he states.

"That is how I see it," I turn around. "People either don't enjoy their lives or wait for the moment they feel is the right time to enjoy it. I am not waiting. You are half way through your life, would you say you're enjoying it?" He shoots back a blank, stupidity - for - asking stare. I put my dishes in the sink and begin to wash them.

"Did you know that I love candles? But I rarely light them because I feel like I'm saving them for some special occasion? Like, I'm saving them for a potential moment in time where I deserve to enjoy them, but right now is not that time. Something that I love and can't wait to use just sits there, collecting dust and I don't get to enjoy it. Six months ago, I started lighting my candles and using my pricey lotions and perfumes. I learned to appreciate them. Things we love are right there in front of us. Sometimes we attain them, but we don't use them. If you don't use them, then you're not living. So guess what I do? I light a candle every night for the one hour I have time for to maybe watch television. I use my lotion and spritz of Chanel and by just doing those two things, it helps me feel like I'm living my life," I lecture.

"You sure talk a lot," he indicates.

"I have a lot to say," I declare.

"I can see that," he says.

"I have a question for your "Mr. CEO," I quote, "You work for yourself, are you even happy at your own job?"

"I don't get to decide if I am happy or not. I still have to go to work," he answers.

"That's not my question. My question is, are you happy at your job? Where you are your own boss, managing your own company for thirty plus years. Just answer the question. Are you happy?" I ask.

He leaves the dining room table and is headed for the kitchen. He opens the top cupboard reaching for a toothpick to pick his teeth. "No," he simply responds.

"Were you ever?" I asked.

"At one point, I was. But now, I'm not," he replies.

"So why don't you change that?" I ask.

"Because I'm in my fifty's and I already have an established business. So what that I hate it? I have to be there anyway. Ok. Nice talk. We're done for the day," he responds.

"This is not a therapy session. This is just a conversation. One last question and I promise to let you go," I propose.

"What?" he asks as if I'm bothering him, but I don't care.

"If you could do anything in the world, what would it be?" I ask.

I love asking people this question. This is how I always decided how to pick my next internship. I took internships seriously. I was interested in learning, but I was more intrigued to work in a field that captivated me. I wanted to work for a magazine, so I did. I wanted to work for Mercedes Benz Fashion

Week, so I did. I wanted to execute events for luxurious department stores, so I did. I ended up in a medical field, that I was not interested in but it led me here so I am thankful. Thinking about leaving my jobs, I was once again excited to dive into a profession that I was passionate about. Where I could be creative and see the impossible be possible, if possible.

He presses the button to the elevator and turns towards me while he waits. "I would do something with travel, I guess. I like looking up flights, hotels and reading reviews. That's interesting to me."

I never thought that was something he enjoyed doing. "So, you should do it," I say.

"I can't," he grunts.

"Why not?" I ask.

The elevator door opens and he steps in. "Because I have to go to work. See ya later." The door closes between us. That was it. The conclusion. You could be half way through your life and still be unhappy at your job.

Working consumes the largest percentage of our daily lives. This is when you need to decide what is most important to you. Is it everyday happiness or continued unhappiness? Unhappiness may support your family financially or your online shopping habits, but once you make the decision to be happier in your everyday life, you will find what is most important to you. Where do we find it? We find it within ourselves.

Jumping Ship

I continue taking my time as I finish up to leave for work. I take notice along my drive of the rows of palm trees and the sun rising above the ocean's horizon. I manage to arrive to work early and in a peaceful state of mind. I pray that today will be as calm as my parallel demeanor. What more could possibly happen besides the building burning down from this summer heat? I scroll up and down my inbox staring over the same minimal answered emails. I'm actually hoping for a new email to pop up so I can reverse this monotony. Spinning my mouse in circles, I track the minutes that have passed and it's only been two. This is the first time since I started working that I actually had nothing to do. I never thought I would get bored of boredom in the workplace. How boring. I hear the vibrational rhythms of my phone pulsate against my desk and instantly reach for it, hopeful for some friendly entertainment.

A text message flashes across my screen that shocks me to my core. The phone falls out of my grip echoing a loud noise when it hits the surface. I again read who it's from, to make sure I am reading the name correctly. It's like the universe put a pile of shit in one basket. Right when I thought it reached its capacity, the universe decides nope; I have one more piece of shit to add. Merry Christmas. And that is what he was. Another piece of shit in my basket.

"Hey stranger." It reads. Fucking stranger? Fuck you. I gave ALL of myself to you. We are not strangers. Of course these are my initial thoughts until I remind myself that King Kong took the day off and I promised to relax today. There must be some type of solar or lunar eclipse messing with my vibes that I cannot have one calm day in this hurricane of a week. Hurricane Brittany, Category Five, has officially arrived. World, take cover.

Background story:

I had this friend who was just a friend, and nothing more. There is such a blurred line when it comes to relationships, especially a relationship formed from a friendship. I was naïve and didn't see his feelings for me that went unnoticed for approximately ten years. Growing up, I was surrounded by male specimen being the only female of all my cousins, including my brother. Therefore, my first thought when I receive attention is, "Oh you want to be my friend because I'm awesome? I would agree with you, I also think I'm awesome."

I've known this friend since I was fourteen years old. I only know this because he made it a point to remind me, constantly. He informed me of the first time he laid eyes on me, sitting next to his best friend and mother, watching me dance on stage for a performance. He asked them, "Who is that girl? I need to meet her." He claims we did not meet until one year later. He noticed me first, but I didn't remember him. Now, ten years later, he leaves a scar in my emotional powerhouse.

Flashback to me, at age twenty-three, I was planning to leave for my first trip to London before New Year's Eve. For weeks, he begs to take me out before my travels, and I finally agree. I could not have predicted that this night would transform into a confession of his desires for me.

Once he made me perfectly aware that he saw me as more than a friend, he asks, "Do I have permission to kiss you?" At first, I think, no. I'm not into you that way. But then I figured, what if I tried this as an experiment… to see that even though I'm not attracted to you, even though we are total opposites, is it possible for me to force myself to have feelings for you? I know, force is a strong word, but unfortunately at first glace, I see guy's muscles before their brains. This time, I wanted to see if I had the room to give his heart and mine a chance.

I accept his offer and allow him to lean in for a kiss. The movement of his hands, the way he coddles my back and thighs, wasn't the hands of a boy. They were of a man. I was accustomed to being with boys. His over maturity, which I had previously condemned, flipped my off switch - on, to fall deep in the romanticism of this starry night. We share the same age but rarely share the same mental maturity, until this moment of intimacy and I find myself fond of his affection.

I admired the dark features of his eyes, his soft, coiffed hair and scruffy face. My body fit perfectly in his, while his height towered over mine. I warmed up to his corny jokes and spontaneity for adventure, hopping on a jet ski at 6:00 PM to watch the sunset. Days turned into weeks, weeks turned into months and I saw him often. I fell for the side of him that was most authentic and tore down my walls to let him in.

My experiment was working. I found myself naturally starting to develop stronger feelings for him. Yet, somewhere along the way, it fell flat and I knew something was wrong. Girls have majorly unapologetic intuitions and if we sense smoke, we know there's a fire. His behavior was off and in every excuse of his words, I began to sense a lie. Within every picture I could see, I uncovered a flaw. I came to discover that my intuition is never wrong. I unveiled he was indeed two-timing me with my friend's younger sister and I out of all people, was not going to let him get away with it.

I discovered I was first a confidant, then a lover turned mistress. I was confronted at my gym about the other relationship I had suspected, and it was confirmed. I let it blow up in his face since my reputation was affected by being known as the "other woman". He didn't reach out to apologize until two months later. At first, I contemplated, and then agreed, to listen to what he had to say. I decided instead of issuing him a *Go Fuck Yourself* (middle finger emoji), I would tell him the reasons why he should *Go Fuck Himself* instead. So, I ripped him a new one and I assure you ladies, it will be one conversation he will never forget. After all, he was the one who introduced me to the game of fishing.

I never understood why men love to fish. Waiting around all day on the water to hopefully catch one fish. Then, it hit me. Fishing is a lot like getting women. Waiting all night to hopefully bring a girl home, or less aggressively, at least get her number. But still, there is the known likelihood in fishing that with all of that effort of waiting for the fish to fall for the bait, there is still a chance that you may come home empty handed. But if you don't, you feel lucky, and you try to catch one more fish. Because once you catch one, one is never enough, and if you are lucky enough to catch two, you have exceeded the expectation of the game. This is why men love fishing because their love for the game overpowers their love for the fish.

Fisherman: "Hey stranger."
Brittany: "Hi."
Fisherman: "How's it going?"
Brittany: "Good you?"
Fisherman: "Could be better."

…. Here he waits for me to respond, "What happened?" but of course I don't, selfish fisherman. Whatever your problems are that you may have, are not more important than quitting my job and moving. Want to know what it's like for fish to wait for their bait? Let me show you.

Fisherman: "Got broken up with via text message."

HAHA. YOU DESERVE IT. After ripping him a new asshole for the position he put me in before this, I could care less about his feelings from his latest catch of the day. BRB let me call the wambulance… oh sorry, they're busy.

Brittany: "That's what you get for dating a gold digger." *Sorry, but she was.*

Fisherman: "That's not nice. I'm really bummed out about it."

Brittany: "Well, you get what you pay for… too bad there are no returns."

Fisherman: "Funny. I just can't believe it. I did nothing wrong."

Brittany: "Sounds familiar, but we haven't spoken in a year and a half. What's up?"

Fisherman: "I just realized I haven't spoken to you in a long time. I miss our friendship… so I wanted to reach out and see if I can take you to dinner sometime."

You miss our "friendship?" Sure you do. Why does he deserve any additional time on this earth with me? While my fingers were ready to send an automatic thumbs down, I realized this was the moment differentiating between my old mental reality and my new mental reality. My old reality would have sent a split-second **hell-no**, never giving him the slightest of chances. My new reality forced me to pause and consider a more positive mindset I wanted to sink into. What if I took a different approach by following a more open, forgiving methodology to say my peace, and then, peace out?

Was I over the situation in the past? Totally. Yes. But when it comes to putting someone in their place, I shove that puzzle piece so hard back in its position whether it fits or not – I will make sure it fucking fits. This is how I viewed the situation. Do you deserve to have the pleasure of sitting with me? No. But this time I will allow it because I have nothing more to lose.

Every experience is worth the experience. Whether it is with friendships, or relationships, every person who comes into your life is there for a reason. Good or bad we can all learn from the experiences spent with that person. With Mr. GQ, I was grateful for allowing myself to give him a chance and fall deep into an emotion of mutual intensity. From this experience, my soul grew. Here, I was also thankful for being able to successfully develop a liking for someone who I would have never looked at twice. My soul learned to adapt. I am too adult to hold grudges against people for reasons that should be left behind.

There is always some light in a dark situation; you just have to look through the clouds to find it. I was willing to move the cloud for him. Once I decided, I was ready to bare off the weight I didn't realize was heavy on my chest. I gave him a first chance, and I am ready to give him a second, because if I learned a lesson from the first time, who knows what I can learn from the second.

As I pull up to the restaurant, he walks over to my car to greet me and open my door. What I hated about him most was, above all else, he was always a gentleman. *Asshole*. And he actually looked really handsome. *Jerk*. I think I never really saw him as attractive until this moment, although I don't know why this time is different. Maybe he just got better looking or maybe I'm just famished.

We take a seat in a two-person booth, sitting across from one another. I detect that he is more nervous than I am and note to thyself to take advantage of this when I needed. We talk about everything but the elephant in the room and I realize that maybe we wouldn't discuss it at all. I actually feel okay with that. Maybe this reunion is more of a let's meet and move past this, person-to-person, or I'll drop the bomb when dessert comes, which it won't, because I won't be ordering any. Time was passing by quickly and I was admittedly enjoying myself.

It was early, only half past nine, and following dinner he was not ready for the evening to end. We still didn't speak about our current state of friendship and his ex-girlfriend drama that I didn't want to get into. I felt I was doing a mitzvah seeing him tonight and after dinner my mitzvah was fulfilled.

"Do you want to continue the night and have a drink? I know of a cool place a couple of blocks down, but it's outside," he says.

It's summer. Does he really think I want to sacrifice my eyebrows and bronzer melting off my face in different shades of brown? No thank you.

"I think indoors would be a better choice. I'm trying to think where else is around here," I say.

"Well," He places his hands in his pockets distributing his weight from his heels to his toes, "I have another option."

"What's that?" I ask.

"I don't want to make you feel uncomfortable, and you can say no – it's just an option. I have three great, unopened bottles of wine that were just delivered to my house. I also did some new renovations and would love to show you if you're up for it?" he offers.

ALERT. ALERT. This is where the original Brittany would abort the mission. But then I thought if I had the chance to be the fisher-woman, and dangle the bait in his face, why not take advantage? I looked bomb.com tonight. Let's light up this baby and let the bomb ignite.

"Fine, but I can only stay for an hour."

"Better than nothing. Let's go!" he speeds with eagerness like a little boy on his way to the candy store. Hope he knows ahead of time that my cookies are no longer for sale.

I follow him and we pull up to the front of his house. My heart begins to race as we pass through the iron gates. I park behind him in the circle driveway as he makes way to open my door. It feels like the quietest night with our shoes echoing against the cobblestoned pavement. He led us through the entry way and up the stairs through the back door. "Ladies first," he smirks. I KNOW THE WAY. YOU DON'T NEED TO REMIND ME.

Here it comes. The sinking feeling of regret. You know those rubber bands in elementary school that are rolled into one big ball and are impossible to untangle? That is exactly what my intestines currently feel like. I should not be here. This was too much. I am drowning in my qualms every step I take up the stairs, so much so, that I can't even hear what he is saying. I'm just pretending to listen.

"Take a right," he instructs.

I follow.

This was a bad idea. But that was the point, to push through the discomfort and be submerged in the present. But, ugh, I feel like he's already won now that I'm about to enter his fucking wing of the house.

He opens the French doors leading into his largely renovated bedroom and living room suite. It is decorated beautifully with wooden features, off-white textured walls, a large mirror expanding the room, and natural, balanced symmetry throughout the bedroom. Basically, it should be featured in a magazine. My apartment literally fits into his room. Sad.

"What do you think?" he asks, eagerly.

"It's very nice," I respond.

"Let's go into my other cave," he leads the way into the other room. I sit at the far end of the L shaped couch when he asks what wine I prefer out of the three. I pick the Malbec, obviously. He pours us both a glass and sits two couch seats away from mine.

"Can we cheers?" he asks.

"Sure," rolling my eyes.

"Thank you for agreeing to see me, speaking to me again and for hopefully getting our friendship back on track from where it was. You look very beautiful."

"Thanks," I grin. We touch glasses and drink. I must have downed half the glass in one mouthful. Living in anxious city, I desperately need it.

A moment of silence passes. I glare at the floor as I catch him staring in my peripheral.

"I just can't say enough that I am so happy you're here. I almost thought we would never be in this place again," he mentions.

"Trust me, I'm aware." I took a smaller sip knowing my glass was almost empty. I look at my watch and time is moving slowly. Great.

"You seem different," he identifies.

"Because I am," I reply.

"What's changed?" he asks.

I laugh. "Life." He notices my glass is empty and reaches for the bottle to pour me another. He sits closer to me and I can sense what he's doing. It ain't happening kiddo.

"I'd like to hear about it," he admits.

"You're sitting too close. This distance is no longer permissible to you," I cheer in his direction. "You know, if you would have asked me to meet with you maybe, four months ago, I would not have come here. We," I signal to us both, "would not be here."

He nods.

"I have had a fucking year bro, but it's allowed me to be able to give you the pleasure to sit in my presence, in front of you," I laugh in honesty.

"Do you regret coming here?" he asks cautiously. I can sense him start to fidget again.

"Not yet…just kidding. I don't. Because I don't care anymore," I throw up my hand and cross one leg over the other, "But let's let this be the open communication room while I'm here because who knows if I will ever return to this home design catalog again."

"Open communication room? Oh no, I'm scared," he sips his drink.

"I know you are I can sense it from your body language." His eyes flash open and he almost spits out his wine. "Be careful, you don't want to ruin your pretty new couch," I tease.

"Ok, ok let's just talk about the elephant in the room then," he states.

"Let's," I agree.

"Let me be the first to say that I know I fucked up. I am the reason our friendship is ruined, hopefully salvageable, but that was the last thing I could have ever wanted to happen. I tried to see if I could be that kind of guy who could have it all. How the other jerks of Miami juggle multiple women at one time, which you in no way deserved. It backfired. I deserved that. I couldn't believe I was pulling it off, but it was not me. It was not my character. I don't want you thinking that that person you witnessed was who I was and who I still am because I still care about you a lot. If anything, I would at least like another chance to be your friend and text or call you to say hi, I'm thinking about you, invite you to lunch. I'd rather be in that place than be total strangers like we became," he moralizes.

"As discussed a century ago, I always saw you as the epitome of the perfect gentleman. Never could I have thought when we decided to become romantically involved that you had even the smallest capability to pull off what you did to me. And in your head even though it may have not been as severe as it was in mine, no boy, guy, or man has ever been remotely close to doing that to me in my entire life. For you to be the first out of all of them absolutely blew my mind. It's like I saw you as this perfect guy, who, no offense, I was not even attracted to in an intimate sense. You made it seem like you really liked me and I felt bad for not giving you that chance, so I did. Now I see you as something totally different. Like, everything you told me on that dock about how you've liked me for ten years… you were too intimidated to tell me how you felt… you always wanted this to grow into something more, all of that just seems like bullshit now. So, it's like, how am I supposed to believe anything you say now? But now it doesn't matter because I actually don't give a shit. It makes no difference to me," I wave it off.

He buries his face in his hand and brushes his hair back.

I continue, "You want to be my friend? Why? No offense, again, but I have closer friendships with other people in my life, than I ever did with you. So, I don't know why mine is so important to you. I know I'm great, don't get me wrong, but why do you think you deserve my friendship back?" I ask.

"I am not the person that I was when I acted that way. It was wrong. But I want to fix it. I want to know how I can fix it," he begs.

"Well, while sitting here, I came to the realization that this is your second break up with a girlfriend in a long time, right?" I ask.

"Uhh…" he thinks back, "I guess, yeah, why?"

"Why am I always your first-round draft pick after every break up with your ex-girlfriends?" I ask. His jaw drops in a surprised, stuck facial reaction.

"You're killing me here." He responds with his hands rubbing over his eyelids.

"Sorry this is just too good. Like you don't understand what a week I'm having so everything is just coming out and this roll I'm on is making me feel so great! But answer me. Why am I always your first call?" I ask.

"Because for some reason when it ends, your picture always flashes in my mind. You are at the top of my list. You always have a happy, positive tone in your voice every time you pick up the phone. I can feel your energy on the other side. I can't explain it. It's like the drug I need to make me feel better but in an actual human form. You always find a way to say the right or wrong thing that will always make it better, never worse. Your vitality gravitates me towards you. It's refreshing," he justifies.

"Good answer. Nicely put. Now is this the bullshit talking or the wine?" I laugh.

"You're the worst. I'm done being vulnerable." He sits up to refill our glasses.

"I'm kidding. I'm done being mean. It's taking up too much of my energy," I exhaust.

"Oh why thank you, you're so kind," he responds, "Should I open another bottle?"

"No, that's enough. I have to get going anyway. Time is up, my fee is $300," I smile.

"Yeah, thanks for the therapy session. If anyone needs to be paid, it's me for my emotional beat down."

"Ahh you deserved it," I gather my purse resting it over my shoulder and walk over to face him. He opens his arms for a hug and pulls me in close without letting go. I can feel his heartbeat pulsating against my own. He tucks the hair behind my ear and slowly indents his fingers along my neck.

"I want to kiss you," he whispers with his nose inches from mine.

"You don't have the pleasure of doing that anymore," *Fisherman*, I respond. "You can walk me out though."

He nods as I walk away and takes a moment to follow behind.

We walk through the house exiting to the driveway without a word. He mimics my stride to the car until he opens my door for the last time. "Thank you for meeting me tonight," he says.

"You're welcome. Thank you for wining and dining me," I wink.

"It was my pleasure," he gives me one final embrace. "When can I see you again?" he asks.

I smile and stroke the soft texture of his face. I take a seat in my car and reverse out of the driveway.

I didn't tell him I was going to London because I felt that he didn't deserve to know. I would rather him be shocked and faintly agitated that he didn't hear it from me. He entered my most inner circle, to then be pushed the farthest outside the line. Now he was on the line, being kept at a safe distance. I metaphorically and physically closed my door as I drove away. The doors that were closed I reopened, and the doors that were open, I closed. I tied my hair up in a bun and blasted, "Water under the bridge" by Adele while singing at the top of my lungs proud of how I succeeded recognizing my self-worth, my self-control and forgiveness. I now can heal.

Friday, June 29th:

My alarm sounds. I unfold the covers hiding my face. The sensitivity of brightness from the morning curtains is a harsh one until I look out at the view. I peek through the breach while my eyes adapt to the light and witness the rising sun. I am ending a habitual morning pattern to one of revival where mornings are meant to be cherished, not taken for granted.

I unlock the sliding glass door and push it ajar, taking each step on the cold Jerusalem stone near the glass barrier. I lay down a towel diagonal facing the east, cross my legs, and rest my hands upon my knees. Inhaling the breeze from the ocean, exhaling the wind from the west, I try to focus on empty thoughts by centering on the waves and the ocean air. Closing my eyes, I imagine these soft murmurs cleansing my mind and body, monitoring each breath I've learned to control.

Joe, a yoga teacher at Equinox, instructs his class to sit in this seated position and place our hands over our hearts. Most importantly, breathe. Feel your heartbeat pulsate through your hands with each breath. Feel your body being alive. You are a living thing. He enforces that we only have one body to live in. Only one. You don't get to return it, you don't get to exchange it, it is yours and you own it. What you choose to do with it, how you treat it, how you feed it is entirely up to you. But you are the one who has to live in this body forever. No one else. So, choose to be good to your body.

The escalation of chaos over these past four days is enough to light a city on fire. I have been trying so hard to not let anger be an immediate influence on my senses. To not allow my emotions to overhaul my instincts so that I don't drive myself into a puddle of tears. But, I choose to not care. *I don't care.* That is what I continue to tell myself throughout the past six months. The repetition of these words is what helped my emotional shell harden.

I. don't. care.

Sitting here in tranquility, I reflect on this past week. I recognize my emotions were triggered by feeling chained to fear. I remained close to the fear only to break away, as far as my subconscious would allow. My natural instincts would be to panic, become irritable, and sink at an accelerated rate. But, by being aware of the situation around me, I chose to be calm. Calmness helped me take both feet out, and walk fearlessly in the right direction.

I never felt the need to rewire my innate method of thinking, because this mental build was the only one I identified with. I led with my instincts and natural measures not realizing that altering my approach would take less effort and would be more enlightening. Not until now could I distinguish that the only perspective I was looking through was behind the camera. We look through multiple lenses until we find the picture we like the most. Little did I know by dropping the camera and moving in front of it, would I begin to live my truth, in the present, as myself. Instead of controlling all factors from behind, it led me in front and exposed. This time, I am looking at the lens head on and I am now the muse.

On *Wednesday*, I paraded in black walking into what I predicted would be a battlefield, which it was. Today, I deem it appropriate to wear white, raising my flag and surrendering to all of my realities. What we wear, who we are, is how we represent ourselves and I wanted to start and end the day completely pure. Not like the risky Madonna 'pure' but more like the Pope 'pure'.

Sitting in my chair, staring at an empty screen, I faintly hear a familiar walk proceeding through the hallway. I shift to get a better listen but turn back afraid of what I might find. I know that sound. And I know better than anyone that this is the sound of My Boss's Lulu Lemon pants in the flesh.

I tilt my desktop monitor in the direction of her window to catch a glimpse of her shadow. Her reflection walks across my screen and it is her! I freeze. She doesn't say hello and quietly enters her nook. If I don't move maybe she won't notice. Of course the day I wear white, you can't miss me.

I hold my breath until she closes the door and force to let it out. I have an A+ in confrontation but I'm not sure how I'll survive the day. It is way too early for this and I have not mentally prepared my cross statement in this case. Neither My Office Neighbor nor My BFF are occupying their forts and I have no one to help plot my escape plan.

My Boss: "Hi, please come in."

Shitting bricks. Every step I take towards her office, I replay the memories from my final verdict. I remind myself that today, I take back control of my emotions and that only I can dictate how I feel. I conquer my fear, choosing to walk into the unknown, knowing that whatever I choose to do from this day will only be in the path of greatness. I allow myself to be consciously aware of who I am and what I can be. I will no longer have to worry about measuring my happiness, because my happiness is immeasurable.

I walk into her office, softly closing the door behind me. I choose a new chair to sit in and refuse to meet her eyes until I am settled in the hot seat. I want her to feel my tension and sense my professionalism with this calm expression. I rest back, crossing my legs, and folding one wrist over the other before I release my stare.

"Hi," she begins.

"Hi," I respond.

"How are you?" she asks.

"I'm fine," I reply, unsympathetically.

"Ok. Well, over the past couple of days, I know there has been a lot of hearsay and false information thrown around due to what has transpired. I wanted to know what your thoughts are on it all," she asks.

My thoughts? Cocking my head I try to wrap my 'thoughts' around her question, did we not experience the same natural disaster in this office? I almost wasn't sure if I should laugh at the formality and pretension she brought to my doorstep.

"I know what my thoughts are. I am more curious to hear yours." I retort.

The verity in her eyes starts to crack, forcing her tear ducks to overflow and emotional shield to melt. I do not flinch. She notices. My heart is naturally empathetic in almost every situation but not this one. The amount of hurt that shaded over my heart morphed from beating red to stone cold black. Being emotionally exhausted, you come to a point where your compassion dries up like a raisin. This is how she affected me. I did not want to choose this. I sit still waiting for an explanation hoping she will deliver the most honest answer. The answer that I deserve.

"I am so sorry this happened to you I cannot emphasize that enough. I have not been able to eat or sleep since this has happened and it is eating me up inside. Watching you walk in here and sit without empathy, I can see how bad I messed up. I didn't want you to leave like this. This is why I was against their decision of giving your Desk Buddy your job. You did not deserve this. I failed you as a manager. You asked for help and I didn't give it to you. I know now that I should have done more and I didn't. I should have pushed for you and I am so sorry. I saw you as a daughter and I was happy to see you grow. I am sorry that this pushed you away and I want to find a way to rectify this," she pleads.

That is all I wanted. The answer that I deserved. I wanted an honest apology and I wanted closure. I wanted her to admit to me, the one person who worked directly under her for years, that I was wronged. Over the course of this week I learned each night through reflection that it was easier to be more open and to forgive than to be closed and unable to let go. First with my fellow colleagues in the company, second with the Fisherman, and third with her. I want to be the bigger person and to leave with the respect I have earned.

"Thank you for your apology. I did not want to leave here buried beneath this mess." She nods. "I don't know about you, but I have done a lot of self-reflection and I honestly just want this all to end. I have no feeling left inside of me. I don't know what I'm still doing here, but I would like to leave here in my last days on a high note. That is all I ask," I reply.

"I'm sorry. I never wanted this to happen to you. Especially to you," she expresses.

"I was sorry too, for myself, but now I'm not. I am doing what I need to do and if you can respect my wishes for amity then, let it be," I respond.

"Okay," she wiped her tears.

I stand out of the chair and exit through the door. The main office door. I head straight to the elevator frantically pushing the button as if it would make the elevator come any faster, but it never does. Before anyone catches me in the shadows, I step into the elevator. As the doors close, I back into the wooden panel and close my eyes on the way down thirty-five floors.

Outside. The air on the bench reminds me of the same air I breathe in front of the ocean. The same air I breathe from my car ride along the east coast of Collins Avenue. The breeze comforts me. The water feels like home to me. This wind brushing against my skin feels like energy passing through me, cleansing my body of impurities, and creating space for pure energy to restore.

Before all of this, I was not in touch with spirituality. Now, I am starting to feel that I am on the right path close to finding my purpose. Finding clarity in this stillness, I open my eyes and feel connected to the water. The only force of nature that can put out my fire when I need it. This is the first time I've ev sat outside on a bench, in this park, across from my off can't believe after three years, I never took a break to ap this view.

I leave the bench and look down at my feet to find nothing more than Abe Lincoln himself. Following me everywhere I go in instances like these. 'Hi Robin,' I say to myself. I continue to the edge of the bay facing the sun, breathing in the light. I place the penny over my heart giving gratitude. "Thank you for watching over me. Thank you for guiding me and making sure I am always okay." I toss the penny into the water and turn leisurely in the direction of the office. On this day, the one thing I know is I will not be rushing. From now on, I will only be present.

Friday, July 8th:

My Last Day

"Although the universe may not gift you with your dream on a silver platter, Leo, you will soon see that you are supported and guided toward the place you want to be. You may not wake up one day and suddenly have what you want, but you will receive the resources you need to get it. The rest will be up to you. If you just fantasize about how nice it would be to succeed, then

~~ not achieve your dream. If you take what you receive,

‑‑th it, you will have exactly what you are

pe.

ₑe silver platter was definitely not

have never wanted it to be. I want

nyself. And with the extensive hard

ₐrn that silver into platinum. I had a

239

vision. And with all the resources I amassed, all I needed to do was take an extra step forward and make a decision. It was all up to me, and despite being scared every step of the way, my determination for success overpowered any doubt in my mind of ramification. I was going to London. I was choosing to press the refresh button on my being to experience the greatness that I have the power to become. We all have the potential. You just have to be brave enough to mind it.

Mind the gap, that is.

Rebirth

Just Do It

How many times do we say we're going to do something, and actually end up following through with it? I would say that 99% of the time, we **don't** follow through. But for the 1% of risk takers who **do**, kudos to you. I want to join that 1%.

I can't tell you how many times I have attempted to diet for an upcoming pool party because my bathing suit bottoms were digging in just a smidge. I would set a goal and make a plan for a 6:00 AM work out until my alarm sounds. When that alarm would sound, I would contemplate for half a second, "should I stay or should I go?" Instantly, I would press snooze, hoping for success another day. When that "another day" comes, the choice to get up in the first place still seems so hard, but in reality, it's really so simple. The diet plan was simple. Planning to relocate my life, not so much. This decision is much more drastic, but the more I said aloud, *I am going to London*, I would have to hold myself accountable and follow through. The question of me wanting to go was definite, but we all **want** to do things in life. The majority of us are just too afraid to **do** it.

Why do I deserve to take this break from life and hop over the pond? Why do I deserve to go anywhere in the world? The amount of times we deliberate the idea of deserving on replay is the moment we psyche ourselves out of doing it. At the office, I felt I had to justify the reasons for personal spontaneity to antagonists who opposed my case. I received a lot of backlash from the older working generation for wanting to take this break after working only three years and cutting cold turkey. Sometimes that's never enough for them but it's not about them. It's about us. Why shouldn't we be allowed to take a break even when we are this young? I think the senior working generation thinks that they never got this chance. That it was not offered to them, so why should us youngens deserve it? What they don't recognize is that breaks are not offered to anyone. A break is as choice. You choose to take it or you don't, and if you don't, guess what? You lose it.

I knew I had overly exhausted myself working so that money would rise quickly in my reservoir. Because of this self-sabbatical income, I was financially able to put my plan into motion. But I still felt that I had to justify to myself why I was going. Apologetically, it is just who I am. But this perception needed to change because I should never feel bad about working hard and investing in my happiness.

It has become more common than not for young adults to leave the corporate world and venture off to find themselves, or their life's next inventive business idea built from passion. Twenty-somethings are becoming a force of self-inspirers who aim for self-fulfillment to drive their self-purpose, not money. They create their own online businesses so they can travel the world guided by their happiness and goals. They teach surf classes full-time in Hawaii, and weave sandals in Greece. For them, this newfound happiness is what fuels their present-daily life and they have paved the way for the 'not thought possible' to be 'possible' by finding how to make it work just by ***doing*** it.

To think that exactly one year ago, I went on a spontaneous trip to Israel that I did not anticipate going on. That I then fell into the deepest love I didn't know existed and planned to move countries for another human, still boggles my mind. One year later, here I am in a new transition *slash* cluster fuck of joy still going along with my plan. Plan A was moving to Israel for a guy, where my life would change for him. Plan B is to move for myself and to change my life for *me*.

On my road to Plan A, I learned selflessness, to give up everything, to be everything, for another. With Plan B (for Brittany) I'm learning to be *self-ish* by being everything for my*self*, which I find perfectly okay. We associate the word selfish with negative implications, but who gets to decide that selfish is a negative word? Is it something we inherited from society pressures during childhood? Or is it an association we determined individually on our own? For me, being *self-ish* is positive. That working on my*self* and being everything I need to be for me, is okay. That I am allowed to make myself a full priority for the sake of my own happiness. That my time is sacred and how I choose to use it is entirely up to me. That if have to be *self-ish* in order to work on my*self*, then being *self-ish* is a right fit for me.

I was choosing this life and I was choosing to be *self-ish* with it. We are allowed to be *self-ish*. These years of our twenties are **OUR** years. Why do we feel the need to rush to be marvelously successful, find 'the one' to marry, or contract that job that will take you to the top, ten years down the road?

If I had been told years ago that one day I would move to London for a short period of time, I would have laughed out loud. "Yeah right! I can't just go to London because I want to. That is ridiculous," old Brittany would say. But why is that ridiculous? I now know it's not. It would be ridiculous if I couldn't afford it and had immovable responsibilities. But if I could find a way to make it work, it could be made possible.

The evident reason we don't go after what we want and constantly stare at our vision board, or box full of 'places I want to go one day', hoping that 'one day' will come soon, is simply because we are scared. 'One day' won't come until we wo-man up and book a nonrefundable ticket. *Self*-dictionary: **Nonrefundable**: an extreme commitment.

Of course, I am afraid of the possibility of going to London and hating it. Or that I could potentially suffer from boredom being unemployed for the first time. I am afraid I would miss my friends and family at home. I am nervous that I would get lost in the tube station and end up in an entirely different part of the country because I'm directionally challenged. I still doubt myself, even after quitting, and consider that I am making an irreversible mistake. But I recognize I'm not solely afraid of moving, missing home, or getting lost on public transportation. I am strictly fearful of one thing, fear itself.

FEAR

When you single out the word **fear**, is it viewed as a negative or a positive word? The most frequent answer would be negative. Fear is defined as an unpleasant sensation triggered by a belief that terror is around the corner. Fear can be caused by a traumatic experience, or not. It can be used as a manipulation tactic at a young age to keep children beneath the covers from the monster hiding under their bed. As an adult, fear is manipulated by no one other than yourself. I subconsciously manipulated myself not to quit my job sooner because I was scared of the "what do I do next?" question. Now, I tell that question to go fuck itself because I knew by confronting the fear, I now have the power to choose what comes next in my life. My entire childhood I was afraid of the dark. I had a night-light in my room until I was maybe thirteen years old. The scariest part of my night was sitting in the dark before I turned on my night-light. Those five seconds sitting in the darkness was what I feared the most.

If you had to associate fear with darkness or light, which one would you choose? Most likely, you would connect fear with darkness. But why? Is it by its definition that you would make that association or, like the word selfish, does society persuade us to choose darkness? Or did we decide that on our own?

There lies a bridge of fear between the darkness and the light. Not until you decide to cross that bridge will you be able to finally explore the possibility of, *what if*? The thing about darkness is, when the lights go out, all you see is black. Then miraculously, your eyes start to adjust to the dark. Moments pass while you lay awake in the shadows until something amazing happens. Your eyes begin to adapt. What is the aftereffect? Your ability to see. Even if the light is not there, just wait. Be patient. The hand you had not been able to see in front of your face is now clear as day, and darkness is no longer something to be feared.

What is hard for some to recognize and accept is that we, as human beings, can adapt. My father is so set in his ways. Being in his late fifties, he cannot imagine life any other way because he lives through one mindset, the same mindset from childhood. He believes mental reprograming isn't possible for him because it's too late. But it's never too late. Adaptation is all mindset. Once we reprogram the mind, we can alter any thought to change it. Like believing selfish is a negative word, when it's not. Like believing the darkness is negative, which it's not. That belief is all in the mind. The first action in adaptation is to take that step into the darkness, be able to exist in it, and live in the void.

I have heard too many times, that *there is a light at the end of the tunnel*. But my question is, why does there have to be a light at the end? Not everyone is going to see the light. Not everyone completes the path to brightness. If we linger in the darkness to confront the fear, we will no longer be afraid. I want to know what I can become while still in the dark.

Many nights I laid awake in my bed, peeking over my covers to stare at my closet door. I waited for my eyes to adjust, just so that I would no longer be afraid. Only until then was I able to fall asleep soundly. But why was I afraid in the first place? Because the fear filled my subconscious mind before it could see there was nothing there. The eyes may naturally adjust, but the mind does not. The mind takes the most work to reprogram its perception.

Everyone has the ability to shift their mindset at any age if they want to… I'm still working on altering my dad's. He doesn't like change. A lot of mid-life adults don't. "What's the point? I've gotten this far, haven't I? And I'm alright," My dad would say. I would rather welcome *change* than avoid it. There is no hurt in exploring a different view that can be a new addition to yourself. Do I feel that I have changed? Not entirely. But I made the decision to contribute *more* to myself that has in turn enhanced my individuality. I never thought I needed to advance my core or mental being, but by exploring these fears and learning to live in the present, I added more to the list of attributes that make me, me. And I learned to love that about my*self*.

I used to believe from childhood that the only way to achieve success was through making a lot of money. I am there now and I can tell you, it's completely untrue. Achieving financial success did not fuel my internal happiness, but it brought me financial security, so I don't regret that former limiting belief. We are bred to believe that at the age of twenty-five we are supposed to reach an occupational goal of hierarchy. To run our own business, reach our first million, or conquer the CEO designation and that's not the case. Why are we rushing our years to reach a goal that does not need to be reached, right now? Five years ago, I used to believe long-term goals were the way to a larger success, for the decade I was diving into. Now, I see short-term goals as being more realistically attainable.

I recognized this post-Israeli-love-affair when I set myself a short-term goal of a one year move in date, instead of a future five-year plan. When half of that year expired, the short-term goal reduced to six months and the half marathon was all I had left. I sat in the darkness for that twelve-month period and it was difficult. It was challenging. But my eyes adapted and I saw more of an opportune future. That anything was better than the initial darkness I walked into. But I was excited to be able to see what was in front of me. Fear is not something to be afraid of but an excitement to be a part of. I always thought it was a cliché for people to say life is an adventure: live it, breathe it, be it. Life definitely could be, if you choose to make it one.

I choose to not look at this quarter life milestone as a crisis, but to look at it as a solution. To choose not to drown, but to float, and take the time to figure out my next destination. That sink or swim millisecond is the exact moment to acknowledge that we always have a choice to make in **our** lives. **The Quarter Life Solution:** Reflect on where you are in your life. Contemplate. Are you happy here? If not, what would you change? Is this job working for you? Is this relationship fulfilling you? Is this life serving you? Think *self-ishly*. It's okay in these moments to put yourself first. You will find that the only person who can truly make you happy, is **you**.

I am a responsible person. I know I will be a great Jewish mother someday, but I am not willing to sacrifice my free time, Equinox, and TV binge watching just yet. But that is just me. For my friends who are now married with children at this age, good for you. You chose that life. That is what you wanted at this age, not me. I want these years to be **MY** years. The only person who can take that away from me is God. And we talk all the time, and God is like, 'Britt, you do you.' So I'm doing me and it feels fucking phenomenal.

There are times when I feel a little scared. That maybe I don't have the security to stay afloat, but what is wild is that I now see the possibility of more. That I used to live in my own little box but now I choose to live outside of it. I see past the walls and corners of the room, also known as my life, and I can see not a shape but a giant atmosphere of air to break through. I realize I no longer need these walls to keep me safe, paths or bridges to pave my next steps, but that any step I take next is possible, and the right one. This box isn't configured to keep me in, but to encourage getting me out. That tomorrow if I choose, I can get up and leave again for a short or long period of time, not tied down to anything because these are **MY** years. And it doesn't need to stop at thirty. I'm just personally not there yet. When I am don't worry, I'll write another book and tell you about it.

We are all frightened and pressured by society, including our mentors who we call on for support. But we live in a different time. A time where a choice is actually a choice and the leisure is yours to **do** as you please. Keyword: **do**. Nike's motto is "*Just do it*", and I am a Lulu Lemon queen, but even on the days I am too lazy to go outside I tell myself, just **do** it. Why? Because…*why not*?

If we learn to magnify our view, we can see the world as limitless. Possibilities are abundantly endless like the ends of the world. The Earth doesn't stop spinning because of multiple disasters. It continues to move and it heals. It is up to us to choose what could be made possible. No matter what external forces come our way we need to just **do** it. Time doesn't wait for anyone and life passes by faster than we can measure. The only thing you can do to stop it is lather yourself in moisturizer and SPF to stop the aging process, but it still doesn't stop it from happening. You can't stop time, but you can change the way it passes and where you are when the clock strikes twelve.

"You may believe that the only thing you truly need to find success with a labor of love is to want it and to believe in it passionately. You may think that as long as you follow your heart all will be well. However, Leo, you also need to take the practical steps that you would take with any other type of endeavor.

You have to have a strategy, you have to be consistent, you have to work hard; all of this is essential to your success. The passion is important, but that's just one of your most important ingredients in your recipe for success," DailyHoroscope.

I was passionate about moving forward. I was passionate about growing as a person. I was passionate about introducing myself to the essence of fear and discomfort by pushing myself beyond the limits I created. I tackled my goals. I quit my job. I made my quarter life solution. Now all that is left to do is finally book my flight.

I waited for Michelle to give me the green light that her spare room was available. Once she confirmed, I immediately purchased my ticket the following day. The feeling of buying something extremely expensive still makes me anxiously hesitant moments before physically pressing purchase online. I stall. I go over the detailed information a hundred times, while rereading the credit card number, following each digit on the screen with my pointer finger to make sure the numerals match. Then I wait to justify for one last moment, should I buy this? Will I regret this? Maybe. But I wanted it in the first place! [Purchase] and I click that button. [Your purchase has been confirmed]. OMG THIS IS REAL. I am officially going to London! I push through my anxiety and commend my absence of buyer's remorse. I am proud that I have accomplished exactly what I wanted six months prior. I followed my own recipe to success just as the stars led me to. And, it wasn't going to stop here.

After purchasing my ticket, Michelle recommended I enroll in a digital marketing course in London. She had taken it herself. I never thought I would go back to school in any capacity, but the thought of learning something new surprisingly piqued my interest. The course is only four weeks, but will give me a purpose to educationally advance, while building my life abroad.

I have six business ideas I want to explore, documented in the notes section of my iPhone. My goal, upon arriving in London, is to find a nearby coffee shop where I can work like a freelancing local (emphasis on the free). My thought is to use the space as a remote office to deliver six business proposals to myself, detailing the probability of success of returning to the states with a thorough business plan. I saved up enough money so that if one of my ideas requires a large sum, I would be able to invest in myself. But only if I think the idea will be 100% successful would I do it.

I keep in mind that if all my proposals lead to failure and I leave London with nothing to show for it, it would be okay. I would be happy knowing that at least I tried and I would start on my next step, finding another job in Miami that values my background in events and marketing.

Michelle prepped a catalogue of essentials I should add to my packing list, so I start to write down the necessities of what I need to buy beforehand. Tampax Pearl is five times the amount in London compared to the price at home. And we all know, we don't substitute Tampax Pearl for anything else, unless it's an absolute red sea emergency.

I start packing my heavy-duty suitcases while fluctuating between outfit choices that are London appropriate, also known as shades of black, grey, and nude. The high stacks of clothing on my bed and long alignment of shoes on the floor ignite overwhelming feelings I cannot shake. This reminds me of the night before leaving for college. My room looked like the stock room of Bloomingdale's, with piles grouped by the hundreds. It was a transition in life I knew I should be so excited for, but I became instantly dispirited when I thought of leaving home. The same experience is occurring now, as I pack for another life transition.

These are the moments when I consider my mother's guiding questions, asking if I am making the right decision. But this time I can't ask, for I don't want her to know I am having any second thoughts whatsoever. I know that if I showed an inkling of fear, she would share one hundred times more of it and I wanted to overcome this on my own. This is the reason why I never left home to begin with. This feeling of discomfort. The feeling that comes out of nowhere, hits you in the face, and shuts down your central nervous system. I converse in my head, how can I bring myself out of this? How can I get out of this funk? Aware of my uneasiness, I lie on my bed and shut my eyes while tears begin to dampen my cheeks. I'm homesick before I have even left. How am I going to get through this?

I think of what yoga Joe once said, to place my hands over my heart. I give myself a pep talk, "It's going to be okay. You are going to have the best time. You will be with your best friend, Michelle. It's only for two months. You love London and they have an Equinox. Equinox is home."

Can you see why I never went to sleep away camp and why I religiously convinced my mother to pick me up at sleepovers at midnight because I could not be away from home? Horrible separation anxiety. It's because I'm a Leo (so they tell me). I hype myself back up by visualizing Michelle and I having the time of our lives in the British lands. I place my palms on top of my bedspread as I lift myself up to continue packing, my hand falls upon something hard that leaves an indentation on my finger. As I gaze down at my covers, I find a penny, randomly tucked into the fold of my pleat, heads up. NO WAY. I immediately think of Robin, "Thank you, I needed that." Feeling her spirit, I know that this decision is the right move and I empty all doubts of opposition. Packing through the newest, strongest transition of my life, she is right there with me. I plant a kiss on Abe's face, I can sense he's blushing. I zip the penny into my duffle bag so I can carry Robin with me on this journey. Besides knowing she would look after me, I also knew she would also look after my duffle bag filled with shoes.

Sitting on the plane is when it hits me that this is really, *really* happening. All I can think of is – I fucking did it. I am that 1%. The plane prepares for takeoff as I reach for my sleep kit of earplugs and a night mask. All I really need is a little lavender essential oil spray, but I'm not that fancy. The moment the plane ascends into the air, I realize it is just me, my baggage, a duffle full of love and Abe. And I'm finally no longer afraid.

There is nothing like waking up from a red eye to a fresh plated breakfast in front of you. I totally don't mind airplane food. Probably because I like all food. But when I smell freshly baked muffins, and this Jew can sniff a hot bagel from a mile away, I'm instantly filled with joy. We land on the tarmac and after the quickest security checkpoint and baggage pick up, I gather my mini U-Haul of luggage and hop in a car to finally meet Michelle.

As the car pulls away from the airport I cannot help but think how, in two weeks, I will be celebrating my twenty-fifth birthday in London. The exact age, at which I predicted three years ago, I would reflect on my life and make a change if needed. It was needed alright. And as I sit in the back of a London car looking out through the trees and cottages, I pinch myself a million times over not believing I am actually here. I did it.

LONDON TOWN

This is the first time in a long time that, when I take a deep breath, I actually feel free. My internal being feels lighter, and I can't help but beam at my smile in the reflection of the window. The smile of genuine happiness that I have missed wearing for so long. I have a lot to look forward to and I'm excited to experience a new, fresh start of independence.

"We are here," informs my driver as we pull into the flower filled corridor of Michelle's apartment. There she is speedily running towards the car as I open the door and almost tackle her in excitement. We roll my entourage of baggage into her building and up to her apartment, where both of us can't help but jump like little girls. We can't believe what we fantasized over many months has finally become a reality.

Walking around her apartment, I immediately feel at home. I was only staying here for a few nights before I move into Josh's six-bedroom house where a room waits for me. I'm so excited to get settled and jump start my tube and walking in the opposite line of traffic tutorial. Her apartment is gorgeously quaint. White walls and dark wood floors complement the gorgeous kitchen with the most beautiful décor. She has flowers waiting and candles lit, as this chick knows nothing more than how to be inherently chic.

I am most thrilled about being able to adventure this chapter with her. Michelle is someone I truly admire. She is effortlessly flawless and ambitious. A girl who is unaware of her beauty, biological generosity, and earnest potential to take over the world. We have been connected for the majority of our lives due to our early hobby of dance. In our bubble, every mother enrolled her daughter into dance school to see whether she had rhythm. Some did, some didn't, but fortunately we did, initiating the foundation of our friendship. Then she hit a growth spurt and even though we were the same age, she was transferred to the tall community, and the short kids stayed together. I was obviously one of the shorty's. Still am, but there's always that *one* short girl in a group and that *one*…is still me.

I make myself comfortable on her white leather couch, looking through the floor-to-ceiling window at the London Eye and Big Ben. I can't believe she gets to look at this view every day. She sits across from my seat searching my eyes to decipher if I'm on the verge of falling asleep, or if she has a few more hours before my jet lag fully kicks in.

"Ok, honest check-in. Do you want to take a quick nap and go out for a nice dinner later, or do you want to try to stay up as much as you can and go outside?" she asks.

"What do you recommend we should do?" I ask.

"It's up to you! I am just so happy to have you physically here," she jumps in her seat.

I look outside and the weather is too perfect to stay indoors. I am in London! I no longer have an excuse to stay inside when I have a whole city to see!

"Let's go outside! The jet lag hasn't hit me yet, but first I have to wash my face and change," I sniff my sweater… airplane smell. The worst.

"Awesome! I'll make you an espresso. I have the cutest place in mind to go for lunch," she recommends.

We walk leisurely through her neighborhood until we reach Sloane Square. We cut through side streets that expose the cutest identical white townhouses with textured doors and black iron gates. Floral pots hang from every lamppost and front doorsteps of each residence. The scent of flowers follows us through each passing street we ease. The town is blooming and alive with locals running their errands, indulging in afternoon tea, and starting happy hour early at 3:00 PM with Pimms in hand.

The air and joyous vibe is fluently easy with a side of exhilaration. Red, shiny double deckers pass our way as we cross the street to another side of the town. All I can think about is how eager I am to ride that bus! Some may not be a fan of public transportation, but the red double decker looks like a Universal Studios Harry Potter ride to me. London Land it should be called. And I am in it.

Michelle leads us through every part of the city effortlessly, pointing me in the direction of some of my most favorite stores. She is the perfect tour guide and I instantly feel like a proud mother observing the way she maneuvers herself through alleyways and sightseeing shortcuts, like a born Brit! Her quick knowledge of this city makes me feel like I could learn it in no time and that I could one day be her tour guide assistant.

She leads us to a restaurant with outside seating under a pergola that welcomes a cool afternoon breeze. We would be sweating our pours clean if we chose to sit outside in Florida this time of year. Once we sit down, a nice English waiter brings us two glasses of water and bread. Normally, I wouldn't touch the bread at the table because I am always watching what I eat, but I'm also starving and on indefinite vacation as far as I'm concerned. Michelle and I catch each other eyeing the loaves of bread. We look at each other in agreement, "Fuck this, I'm starving!" and rip it to pieces.

"I don't know what it is. I think it's all of the walking here but I keep losing weight. It's not like I'm not eating. I eat a house for every meal. But somehow, the weight just stays off," she adds.

"Oh my God I hope that happens to me. I looked back in my activity tracker on my phone and sometimes I don't even walk half a mile after the gym. That's embarrassing. Maybe something is wrong with the app," I convince myself.

"Must be the app," we jokingly agree.

We spread rosemary butter into the dough, and dip the bread into infused olive oil, topping it with minced olive spread. Since we are Americans, we perceptibly ask for another basket, as one is never enough, especially when we have to catch up on each other's lives.

Michelle is currently residing in London with her boyfriend and is looking to figure out her next professional move. I, on the other hand, am completely unattached while finding my happiness and looking for the same next big idea of my own.

"I want to pick your brain for a second," she proposes.

"Ok, shoot," I listen.

"While you're here… what are your thoughts on collaborating and starting our own type of consulting endeavor, like we've always talked about?" she asks.

Michelle and I have always wanted to work together professionally, but never knew when or how we would do it. Even though I was planning to work on my own business proposals, I am always open to exploring any professional opportunities, if any, were to arise.

"What do you have in mind?" I ask.

"I have a few friends who are starting their own companies and need marketing and social media management. I work for them on a contractual basis and think that both of us have skills that complement each other in different areas of a business. If we work together on similar ventures, I think it would be very rewarding for the both of us. You don't have to say yes or no right now, you just got off a red eye, but let me know what you think," she offers.

"I mean, as you know, I don't really have a set-in stone plan here. I think that was my plan – to have no plan for once," we laugh, "the only sectors I want to focus on are my business ideas which, knowing me, will probably only take a week to complete. And I have a meeting with Equinox next week to see if I am able to teach classes there. So, I'm not saying no, but I'll give you a maybe. You know I am not the kind of person to turn down an opportunity. Once I'm fully settled in, we can visit the possibilities of us!" I raise my water glass to cheers.

"Yes! That is awesome. Obviously, no rush. But I am so happy to have you here!" She enthuses.

"Me too!" I praise.

The next morning begins my training on how to maneuver the tube. It's a lot easier than I thought and I'm thankful. I love the rush of quickly censoring my Oyster card to gain access to the station, while deciphering which route I need to take within seconds to hop onto the right tube. The haste of the Brits getting from point A to point B fuels my excitement and I feel like this is what it's like to be a city girl. The tube is much cleaner and quieter than any subway in New York. New York, no offense, just makes me feel like wherever I walk and the air I breathe is going to give me a pimple by nightfall. Here is very different. There is tube etiquette where everyone minds their own personal space and rides quietly to their destination. If only every airplane in the United States could learn this etiquette, air travel would be such a joy.

Michelle and I walk near the shop that her boyfriend and his best friend co-own on Tottenham Court Road. It is a newly plant-based organic kitchen and café called Rawligion. Great name. I have never eaten plant based, vegan, organic food but I am definitely willing to try it. We turn the corner and enter the lovely storefront with greenery on the walls and an aroma of freshly made coffee. I admire a glass apparatus by the window with coffee slowly dripping into the bottom cylinder until Michelle grabs me to reconnect with Tabby, Josh's best friend and co-owner.

His infectious energy spreads as he reveals his passion for this raw, plant-based lifestyle. I try not to let my drool reach the floor, as we tour the front space and products from smoothies, to juices, to meals, and large amounts of my favorite, desserts. We sit down for a tasting of the menu. This type of food is foreign to me but he convinces that it will be a delight. And my God, it is. If this place existed in Miami, I would instantly convert into a plant-based addict for the rest of my days.

"How is business doing?" I ask. "Can you please transport this to Miami?"

"I wish!" he says, "We're only two-months old but growing, and truly, I need more hands-on marketing and event staff to get us on the map. So I can't transport just yet."

I decide to give Tabby some quick pointers to test out, like social media check-ins, mailing list add-ins, and giveaway entries in return for free chocolate rochers. He was going to toss them out anyway so this chocolate free-be is an instant success. As I continue to give him more tips and tricks on how to enhance a following of customers, he observes and asks if Michelle and I would like an internship with him. At first, I never thought I would be an intern again. But then I think that I like to eat food but don't have credible work experience to showcase it. Maybe this is the universe telling me that Michelle and I should, indeed, work together.

Thinking how I believe in Tabby and want their store to be on the path of reaching its infinite peak of success, I realize, if I could even remotely assist with this, the reward would be greater than the experience. Before accepting, Michelle and I decide to finish our schmoozing in the store and commute over to Soho house to discuss. We use this time to sit and decide that we will form a dual consulting mini-biz together. Rawligion would be our first client towards creating a plan on how we will operate as a team.

Sitting on the rooftop of 76 Dean Street, we order cappuccinos and connect our computers. We create a list of what we feel we can contribute to both our own makeshift enterprise and as interns for Rawligion. We're determined and we're excited. Devising ideas together, I realize just how much I miss being excited about work. Not to mention, I have only been in London one day, and I'm riding the momentous wave this city is graciously gifting me. We make the decision: we will do this. And three days later on Monday, we begin our super cute internship as the badass team we always knew we could be.

I did not expect that only twenty-four hours after touching down in London town, I would land a job and fall back in love with working. And that after five days of breathing the British air, I would attend a meeting at Equinox Kensington, where I am scheduled to teach Dance twice a week. And that one week later, after beginning my digital marketing course, I would apply my newly learned tools to real life conditions at Rawligion.

I can feel in my soul that I am finally on the right path to finding my purpose. I was knocked off the path for so long, it took me to move to another country to realize what I have been missing. Every day feels like a day worth living and everything is happening for *this* reason. If I didn't leave everything behind, it wouldn't have fallen into place so quickly. Trusting the universe was the first step. Trusting myself was the second.

Wherever you are, and whoever you are with, you should always welcome every opportunity. I have always believed if there is a door, don't knock. Open it. If it is open, walk through it. Say hello and close it, if you wish. There is no opportunity that you cannot find and that cannot find you. You just have to be open to it.

Weeks pass by and I am excited to wake up in the morning. I jump out of bed when the alarm sounds at 8:00 AM, happy. I am moving at the natural pace of life as God has designed. I have created my own work schedule Monday through Friday spending my mornings at Equinox and the remainder of my day at Rawligion. Working long hours because I choose to. Working hard because I enjoy to. Being present because I learned to. And most importantly, it has given me a gift I have searched for, for so long. Balance.

My entire being feels whole, light, and spirited. I used to let others control my emotions but now I am the one that fuels it. This is what lies on the other side of the bridge that I was afraid to cross. The fear trapped me into not leaving sooner, but none of that matters now. None of that matters now because I have made it here. I am the 1%. And even though the road was dark, I existed in the void and found my way. Everyone has the opportunity to cross their own bridge, and it's not the end of the road. It is really just the beginning.

I never took risks. I didn't like the thought of leaving things to chance. But the greatest chance I ever took was on *myself*. What will you risk when life gets in the way?